THE ACTIVIST'S TOOLKIT

THE ACTIVIST'S TOOLKIT

Advice and Encouragement from an Experienced Activist
to Help You Be a Successful Leader in Your Community

REX BURKHOLDER

Ideas, inspiration and discussion  *on creating better, smarter cities*

Published by Rex Burkholder, Portland, Oregon
Edited and designed by Girl Friday Productions
www.girlfridayproductions.com

Editorial: Nancy Brandwein
Interior and cover design: Paul Barrett
Cover art: Matt Wuerker

ISBN-13: 9781507897980
ISBN-10: 1507897987

Library of Congress Control Number: 2015902465

First Edition

Printed in the United States of America

CONTENTS

*These useful ideas will help you discover your
strengths and passions and find your place as a
leader in your community.*

*Successful leaders know how to find inner
balance, conviction, and hope; they also know
how to reach out to others for help and ideas.*

YOU, MAKING THE WORLD BETTER

"Start by doing what's necessary; then do what's possible;
and suddenly you are doing the impossible."
—Saint Francis of Assisi

There is no getting around it. Asking people to change how they live isn't easy. The current path is always the easiest even if not always the most desirable. We've been trained to "leave it to the experts" because the experts always know best. And if that's not enough to stop us, we are barraged with discouraging clichés such as "You can't beat city hall" and "What can one person do?"

Is it any wonder that most of us are content with complaining?

It's unavoidable: taking on any problem, large or small, means making a commitment—of time, of energy, and of yourself. And all without any guarantee of success or appreciation. Yet every day, thousands, if not millions, of people around the globe get up and put in the effort to make change happen. How do they do it? What is different about them that they do more than just complain, even taking substantial risks at times, to stand up for their communities? I can see why someone would volunteer to improve their children's schools or to clean up their neighborhood parks. Activism out of self-interest isn't hard to grasp. But what about the old man who plants trees, knowing they won't bear fruit or provide shade until well after he is dead? Or the college student in Vermont who raises money to build wells in Africa so that villagers there have access to clean water? What is it that motivates so many people to get out there and work to make this world a better place or to improve *someone else's* lot in life?

Have you ever asked yourself questions like these?

- What can I do about things that concern me, such as climate change, social inequities, lack of job opportunities for youth, or . . . you name it.
- How do I take an idea to make my community better—like creating a pocket park for meeting neighbors and for kids to play in—and go about getting started?
- When I read about a great project or idea happening somewhere else, how can I make this happen where I live?
- I see and read about stuff happening, but how do I get involved?
- If I get started, will others help? What will it take to get them to join in?

If you have ever asked yourself questions like these, this book will help you take the seed of an idea and plant it so that it grows into a real, viable project. Maybe it will change your block, your school, or your community. Or it might cause a change that reaches across the country or even the globe. I have seen so many wonderful things happen because people had an idea and said to themselves, "Why not here? Why not now? Why not me?" <u>You can do it, too.</u> I know, because that's how it happened with me. But first, I think it's important that you know something about who is dispensing advice, so here is my story . . . and the stories of people who have inspired me in my work and life as an activist.

MY STORY . . . AND STORIES OF PEOPLE I ADMIRE

Growing up in the United States during the 1950s and '60s. I was taught that self-interest and personal advancement are the main driving forces in life. This was simply the American Way. Even science told us that life was about competition and winning rather than cooperation and helping. As I learned it, evolution was a bloody battle to get to the top of the heap. Yet somehow this didn't seem right to me. I regularly saw people who were eager to help others. Whether working on a community project with the Boy Scouts or helping Mom at the Roadside Settlement House, I found a lot of joy and fulfillment when I worked with others to do good. Likewise, when I got older and planted trees with Friends of Trees or advocated to make Portland bicycle friendly or simply picked up a rake and helped my elderly neighbor with her yard work. None of this advanced my genetic line or made me richer in monetary terms. Was I an economic and evolutionary failure?

Since those long-ago days when I was a schoolboy, there have been major changes in our understanding of how evolution really works. Scientists have recognized that evolution is NOT a bloody struggle for individual supremacy but is about ensuring the continuation of a species as well as the habitat it depends upon. *It turns out that cooperation, more than competition, really determines which traits get passed on—that is, who is successful.* Think about it. Individuals exist only for an instant in time. None of our achievements mean anything unless we pass them on. If we don't share our love for our fellow humans and fellow creatures, all of our work to improve ourselves through education, making a bunch money, or achieving self-actualization is meaningless. Poof! Here today, gone tomorrow.

Evolution teaches us that our legacy is passed along only through engaging with community and making a difference in the lives of others. And there is a lot of difference to be made. Here are three stories of ordinary citizens who are making a difference:

- Kayse Jama spent fifteen years moving from country to country after fleeing a war-torn and dangerous Somalia, eventually landing in Los Angeles. There he slept on the floor of a Somali restaurant, where he washed dishes in exchange for getting something to eat. He later moved to Portland, Oregon, following other Somali refugees there. The day after he arrived, he was driving a taxi to the airport, even though he didn't know where the airport was! Then 9/11 happened. There was incredible anger against Muslims, people who looked "Middle Eastern," and immigrants in general. Kayse brought together people from his mosque and others around Portland and organized an interfaith gathering to, in his words, "counter hate with knowledge," reasoning that people can't hate others if they actually know them. Out of that grew the Center for Intercultural Organizing, which works to defend immigrant rights, but even more importantly, helps immigrants become true citizens by teaching them how to be involved in their new communities. To serve on committees. To volunteer at their children's schools. To register to vote, and, someday, maybe to run for office.

- Raised in inner-city Portland, Oregon, Isaiah, like many of his friends, joined a gang. He ran drugs and roamed the streets. At seventeen, he shot and killed another boy. In prison, he met a man, Freddie McGee, who had spent ten years behind bars for his own gang-related crimes. Freddie was the first person in Isaiah's life who challenged him to think about his future. What did it mean to be a man? Did he see a future other than the early death suffered by so many of his friends? Freddie helped Isaiah see what was missing in his life and to look for ways to fill that hole with meaning. Isaiah's outlook and his behavior changed. Offered early release for good behavior, Isaiah choose to stay two more years in prison so that he could finish training to become an electrician, knowing he would need a skill when he got out if he was to do more than return to gang life. But he also pledged to help others as Freddie had helped him. In addition to his day job, Isaiah speaks of his mistakes and revelation to students and gang members, even appearing at TedX talks in Portland. With Freddie, he works with young men on the street, hoping to help them find the meaning in their own lives before they lose theirs, or take another's.

- As for me, I was a thirteen-year-old kid in Des Moines, Iowa, when I started picking up litter on Grand Avenue. It was 1971, and a noble-looking Indian—played by actor Iron Eyes Cody—cried in television ads filled with images of smog, polluted water spewing into rivers, and people throwing trash out their car windows. I was just a carefree kid running around in the woods, hunting crawdads in creeks, and camping with the Boy Scouts, but that day walking down Grand Avenue, a light went on in my head. With cars whizzing by, and other kids looking at me like I was nuts, I started picking up roadside trash.

HOW DID IT START WITH YOU?

Are you someone who's seen something troubling and recently decided to do something about it? Believe me, I know the first baby steps in civic activism can seem pretty daunting—so much to do and so much to know! Those first efforts can seem futile, a proverbial drop in the bucket. What difference does picking up litter along the street make in a world where corporations and cities dump their waste into the very water we drink from? Giving a dollar to a homeless person won't restructure a highly unequal economy rigged to benefit the rich. Turning off the lights when leaving the room won't stop global warming.

So why do it? *Because this is how all change starts.* These small acts are expressions of hope, of humanity, and of love. Sometimes it really <u>is</u> as simple as giving in to a moment's impulse.

I wrote this book as a spur to action, a guide, and a source of encouragement for all budding activists who see the world as it is and feel the urge to make it a better place. It's not about courage; courage will be needed, and will come, later. This book is about finding ways to turn your impulse, your good thought, into action—and then into change.

My solitary morning litter patrol was my first step. It was also the last one I took alone. Caring opens you up to all the others out there who also care. They are invisible until you take that first step. Then you will be astounded by how many people there are who care about the things you care about. People who can help and mentor you, who will open up new opportunities for action or just help you fold envelopes or make phone calls or maybe even pick up soda cans with you. My odyssey started when one of my junior high teachers noticed my concerns and asked me to help organize the first Earth Day event at my school.

In this book I share what I've learned over forty years of civic activism. As a citizen and parent, as a professional advocate, as an elected official, as a human who wants to make a difference. I've learned how to go from complaining about the failures and shortcomings of the world to engaging with it and changing it for the better. I am still amazed, looking back, at what has happened in my community because I took that first step:

- Portland has become a mecca for bicycle riding, from just a few "crazies" like me, willing to bear danger and scorn, to almost 10% of commuters using this environmentally friendly, affordable, and healthy transportation today. Our air is cleaner, our roads safer, and our community friendlier today because a few people had a vision and cared enough to do the work to make that vision real.

- Once nearly abandoned, Portland's inner-city neighborhoods today are thriving, exciting places to live, attracting thousands of people, young and old. I helped in ways large and small—volunteering at our neighborhood school as well as leading the regional government to stop sprawl and encourage inner-city redevelopment. I campaigned for funding of parks and greenspaces in the city. I also passed a new fee that raises over $1 million a year to give urban kids access to nature through Outdoor School.

- Social justice and sustainability advocates came together in an unprecedented alliance to move the civic agenda in a new, progressive direction. We agreed to speak honestly and openly to each other, across barriers of race, class, economics, and interests. The group I cofounded changed how our community talked about issues, bringing forgotten and ignored voices to the table and giving them real power.

WHAT TO EXPECT FROM THIS BOOK

This small book is not a management book. It won't tell you how to write a grant application or get a meeting permit. Those details are easily taught and easily learned. Instead it's a toolkit stuffed with tools you can use to:

- Discover what motivates you to become an activist and how to take those first steps to transfer your passion into action.
- Understand your role as a leader and develop the skills that will enable you to get others to join you.
- Find coaches, advisors, funding, and other resources to support you in your journey as an activist.
- Get rid of the blinders of common sense, privilege and power, and expertise and false notions of brilliance.
- Learn how to really listen to others—especially those who are "other" than you—and swap stories to work together effectively for change.
- Survive your first meeting—from tapping the knowledge of other leaders in the room to knowing when to break out the beer and pizza.
- Find a trusted local guide to help you understand the perspectives of people who are crucial to your campaign but who you have not engaged with before.
- Drill down to find the common values you and "the haters" share so you can build a platform on shared values and passions.

- Discover the best way to ask for what you want—whether it's playing nice, being prickly, or using a combination of both techniques.
- See failure the productive way and call it by what it is, a milestone or a lesson that can teach you better ways to achieve your goals.

I have woven two features throughout the book. Some are exercises I call TRY IT NOW, in which you have the chance to try out some of the ideas we discuss and put them into practice. And others are called FROM THE TRENCHES, stories of lessons learned either by yours truly or other experienced activists. Some are cautionary tales and some are examples you might want to emulate. Look for them. I hope you will find them particularly helpful and something you can refer to, maybe even share with others you work with.

There is much to do to make this world a safer, more just, and healthier place for everyone. Each and every day is an opportunity for you to act. Even so, problems will appear too big, too complicated, or too messy to fix. People will give you a hard time for caring. So what? There are so many actions we can all take—a torn sleeve that needs mending with a stitch or two, a phone call to make, a check to write— that will begin the healing process.

Like a wrench or screwdriver or search engines or whatever you pull out when you have a problem to fix or a question to ask, *The Activist's Toolkit* will give you the tools to bring together people, ideas, and organizations in powerful ways to make a real difference in your community. Go for it!

"TRY IT NOW" EXERCISES

"FROM THE TRENCHES" STORIES

CHAPTER I

WHY WE BOTHER: PLANTING SEEDS OF CHANGE

"Unless someone like you cares a whole awful lot,
nothing is going to get better. It's not."
—*Dr. Seuss,* The Lorax

What motivates you, gets you out of bed in the morning, and causes you to go to work so you can keep your family fed and warm? Love. It's also what gets us involved in our churches, in political campaigns, and in our neighborhoods. Love is why we check in on our elderly friends, why we sweep our sidewalks, and why we report suspicious behavior. It's hard to believe, but love is even the reason why we attend evening city council meetings. It might seem odd to talk about love in this context. But what would a city be without love?

Because my activism takes place in a city I love, Portland, Oregon, you will be hearing a lot about Portland and the initiatives I've worked on to effect change there. You may have watched *Portlandia*, the popular spoof of Portland, starring Fred Armisen and Carrie Brownstein, which includes a recurring sketch about Portland's over-the-top activists, from lovers of free-range chickens to fanatic bike advocates. Although I've never met anyone who wanted to know the name of the chicken that produced the eggs they were eating, Portland *is* a city full of activists, young and old. I'm somewhere in the middle, so let me tell you my own social change "love story," to inspire you to star in your own. It's a story of ups and downs, of false hopes and real progress—like all love stories! And, like tales of true love, it's a story about long-term commitment.

THE PLACE I LOVE

In the late 1970s I moved to Portland, Oregon, a smallish city on the western edge of the North American continent. Once a prosperous gateway to the riches of the Northwest—fur, timber, gold—the city had fallen on hard times of its own making. Like many other cities in the post–World War II era, Portland adopted policies that essentially gave up on the city as a place for people to live and raise families. Despite Portland's strong school system, comfortable neighborhoods with stately homes, and plentiful parks, city leaders took many actions that made living in the city harder. They promoted massive freeways that displaced tens of thousands, cut the city off from its riverfront, and fueled sprawl and white flight. Stately old buildings were torn down, replaced with surface parking lots to accommodate suburban commuters. So-called urban renewal projects displaced lower income and ethnic communities. Policing and other urban services were deliberately diverted from neighborhoods where African Americans were forced to live. Most African Americans lived in an area called Albina, which had lost forty thousand residents during the 1960s due to freeway building, block busting, and other actions. If you could come up with the money, stately mansions in the inner city could be had for less than $25,000, a more modest home for less than $5,000.

For a young wanderer like myself, Portland was an incredible bargain. My first home was a room in a grand old six-bedroom house in Northwest Portland—it cost me twenty-five dollars a month. But beyond cheap housing, there wasn't much else to attract people or investment. Portland had a small, mediocre public university, a dying downtown, and a city government recently rocked by grave corruption scandals that had brought US attorney general Robert Kennedy to town in the early 1960s.

While working a traveling job for the Forest Service, I met Lydia, my future wife, in a music club in Seattle. We followed her teaching career back to Portland. We bought a home close to her school in one of those neglected and dismissed neighborhoods and discovered something quite unexpected—a group of people who hadn't given up on their city and, against all economic arguments and opportunities to leave for the suburbs, had stayed. Our new neighbors told my wife to walk down the middle of the street at night, for fear of muggers in the bushes. Carrying a golf club was a common practice as defense against the occasional unchained watchdog. A roommate of ours once showed up at work and found a murdered man in the doorway of his cabinet shop. Every child at our local school, where Lydia taught, got free lunch because their families lived below the poverty line.

Yet the same neighborhood was the site of one of the earliest integrated neighborhood associations in the city. Working together, neighbors created a new park next to the elementary school that had only a blacktopped yard for the children to play in. They organized tree-planting days to replace aging street trees and neighborhood cleanups to get the rubbish out of yards.

And why would they do this? You can only call it love. These people saw a community that had been a good place to live and raise a family deteriorating into a crime-ridden, derelict district. They decided to do what they could to reverse this decline, even if they didn't have the support of the politicians or bureaucrats. They had a vision of a community where neighbors cared for each other and the place they lived. They reached out. They organized. They accomplished things. And they succeeded in transforming a forgotten place back into a vibrant neighborhood, verdant with new trees and parks, ringing with the sound of children playing, and enticing shopkeepers and restaurant owners.

Love's strength rescued this community and protected it during renewed hard times. In the late 1980s, southern California gangs, the Bloods and the Crips, expanded their drug dealing operations to Portland. They moved into neighbor-hoods with high numbers of African Americans to avoid police detection. Despite a murderous turf war that at its peak killed almost three hundred people in a year, the Portland Police struggled to come up with an effective strategy to control either the drug dealing or the gun battles. Many in the African American community feel (even today) that slow police response was a continuation of the neglect of the years before, as well as an indication of institutional racism in the police department.

Once again, it was the community that stepped up. Led by people like John Canda of the North/Northeast Neighborhood Association, Ron Herndon of the Black United Front, and Bishop A. A. Wells of the Albina Ministerial Alliance, they organized citizen patrols that went out into the night, creating a presence on the street to fill in when the police weren't around. Tony Hopson created an organiza-tion called Self Enhancement Inc., a mentor program focusing on reaching low-income African American youth—before the gangs could. They created viable and attractive alternatives to joining the many gangs active in the neighborhood. Tony persuaded the city to give up one corner of the city park with the highest level of drug dealing and gang shootings to build a community center where youth and their mentors could safely get together. To do their homework. To play basketball in a safe place. To meet successful local role models who offered them a place in a caring community.

Why would ordinary people put on bright orange vests, walk the night streets carrying only flashlights, and confront young men most likely armed with guns? The only answer I can come up with is love.

TRANSFORMING LOVE INTO ACTION

It Starts with Knowing Yourself

It might surprise you when I say that the first step an activist should take is NOT to take one. Sounds like something a Zen monk would say. Yet, in today's amped-up, plugged-in, and overscheduled world, it's a struggle to find the time and mental space to think about your life and what you want to do with it. We are constantly bombarded by demands for our attention, with little downtime to just space out, as well as lots of guilt (I'm being unproductive!) if we do. Wouldn't it be great if we all took a class in high school that gave the assignment Discover Your Purpose in Life, due in six months? No reading, no homework to turn in. Just think!

Traditionally, many societies used various spiritual and religious practices to center their new members in the community. While many of those practices were on the lines of "follow these rules or suffer," there were also practices that were intended to wake up the moral and social conscience. In Native American societies of the Northwest, young men would set out alone on vision quests, spending a few days in isolation, often with no food, and wait for what would come to them. In the Columbia River Gorge near Portland, you can still see rough pits dug into the volcanic rock exposed to the blazing sun and cold rain. What the young men expected, and would usually experience, was a visitation from a creature they took as their totem and spiritual guide. The vision quest included—and this is crucial—spending time before and afterward with tribal elders who would guide and interpret the experience, in this way helping the young people find their adult roles in their community.

In Australia, young Aborigines embark on a "walkabout" that is very similar. Separated from family and clan (imagine how hard this must be when you've spent your whole life in a community of fifty or so!), the youth wander from holy site to holy site pondering who they will be and how they will serve their community.

Such experiences are rare in modern industrial society: in Europe, some students embark on a *Wanderjahr* or gap year between high school and university, but these are usually unguided explorations of quasi-adult living. True, they occur away from family, and though they come with programs and other resources that provide housing, they lack the purposeful attention of experienced guides who can help the students find purpose and roles in their communities. In the US, programs like Outward Bound reach a small set of the privileged or the troubled, but in general we are uncomfortable talking about civic responsibility and human purpose.

Civics education—that is, how to be an authentically engaged actor in society—was abandoned in the US during the 1960s in reaction to the suffering caused by the excesses of nationalism worldwide, whether communist, imperialist, or fascist. The 1960s also saw a growing rejection of corporate culture and a distrust of the military-industrial complex with its propaganda in support of foreign wars and domestic conformity.

Chances are no one other than a high school counselor or your parents ever asked you, "What are you going to do with your life?" It is very rare to have been led through exercises to discover what is important to you and to understand why. (Your parents telling you to get out of bed and get a job doesn't count!)

When was the last time you asked yourself, "Why do I do what I do?" Think about your last conversation with a new acquaintance or an old friend. You probably went over intimate details of job, family, and health, maybe even some juicy gossip, but did you or your friend inquire as to why you were doing, doing, doing? In the preface I presented a list of questions. Let me repeat them here:

- What can I do about things that concern me, such as climate change, social inequities, lack of job opportunities for youth, or . . . you name it?
- How do I take an idea to make my community better—like creating a pocket park for meeting neighbors and for kids to play in—and go about getting it started?
- When I read about a great project or idea happening somewhere else, how can I make this happen where I live?
- I see and read about stuff happening, but how do I get involved?
- If I get started, will others help? What will it take to get them to join in?

Think specifically about a question to which you answered yes—whether it was about your desire to improve your community or your concern about a global issue. Based on the previous discussion about finding purpose in life, what would your response be if I asked you these questions right now?

Is this more than a passing concern prompted by the latest news story, or do you feel passionately about this issue?

- Is there a path for you to give something more than a resigned sigh or a Kickstarter donation?
- Can you see committing time, thought, and energy to solving this problem?
- Is there a higher purpose for your life that you could find in doing the work of making change happen?

SHARING YOUR PASSION

Getting other people to help is a crucial part of leading. Imagine that the change you want to make is a product that you have to sell to your friends. Could you talk about it so that they would get excited and want to buy it? You will need their time or their money—and in your life as an activist, you will ask for both! How would you go about asking for them? You'd want to be able to quickly and accurately describe this amazing product, what it is, and what it does. What makes it special and desirable? In fund-raising and sales, people are taught how to create an "elevator speech." Heard of it? It goes like this. Imagine you get on an elevator with your friend. It starts heading up. You have thirty seconds to tell them about what moves you and how you want them to help.

What would you say? What is it that you are doing that is special and worthy of their involvement? Why should they care about your passion? Do this: make a list of the key points you want to get across in that half minute. Then test them out on yourself. Would you be excited to work with this person? Are they doing interesting and important work? Will they be successful? Do they make you want to join in? What would it take to make you want to help out? Remember that people are attracted not just to ideas but to personal passion for those ideas—how you present yourself is as important as your analytical arguments and statistics!

Think of what Gandhi said about the relationship between personal and social change:

If we could change ourselves, the tendencies in the world would also change. As a man changes his own nature, so does the attitude of the world change towards him.

This is often misquoted as something like "Be the change you want to see." But Gandhi was not talking about an inward-looking process. Rather, he points out that how we act, how we express our values and our passions, can change how successful we are in getting others to respond to our desire for change.

The following is the first of several exercises you'll find throughout this book, exercises designed to help you communicate your passion effectively, hone your leadership skills, and more. Each time you see the heading TRY IT NOW, you will be invited to delve in and try an exercise to sharpen your skills and add to your toolkit as an activist.

YOUR ELEVATOR SPEECH:

This technique will help you to convey many kinds of messages quickly and concisely, whether you are making a pitch for action, asking for money to fund a project, running for office, or looking for a job at a nonprofit. The process of boiling down your request into a coherent, compelling message helps you to clarify your own goals and strategies—a good thing to do *before* you go public with your ask.

But what if you aren't so clear about your goals? Don't despair. I had a friend in high school who knew for sure at age sixteen that he wanted to study medicine and become a doctor. I don't know if he achieved that goal, but I do remember being amazed that he had a life plan—at least for the next eight years of schooling. Me? I wasn't quite as focused. Don't worry if you don't know exactly what your future holds. The whole process of life is about change and sharpening focus on what is important and what is not. What you *do* need is some sense of what is important to you to enable you to judge what opportunities and challenges are right for you. Take my own life, again, as an example. While hitchhiking as a young man, I told the man who gave me a lift that I hoped to "change the world." He liked what he heard me say, but then asked me, "Well, what are you actually going to *do* to change it?" I was stumped.

Forty years later I don't know that I have a direct answer to that question. I still wake up asking myself if I am doing enough. Have I really taken advantage of all the opportunities I was given, such as a good education and a happy, supportive family? Still, as I look back, I see that even this vague desire to make the world a "better place" was enough to prompt me to jump in and help when opportunities arose. My hopes and dreams influenced my choices in careers, where and how I live, and even my relationships with others.

TRY IT NOW #1

Creating Your Elevator Speech

Let's create an elevator speech for your cause. There are many ways to do this; here I use a technique called the three Vs, developed by my friends at the Metropolitan Group, a national company that helps nonprofits and government agencies motivate people to action. The three Vs are Values, Value, and Voice. First, identify the underlying Values, like caring for one's family, that your idea would help achieve. Second, pinpoint what your approach will provide in terms of Value, such as a safer community. And finally, clarify how you will engage people and talk about your issue—your Voice—the how being as important as the why.

Here are the three questions I will help you answer:

- **Values:** *What core values are central to your organization/idea and connect you to the people you're trying to engage and serve?*
- **Value:** *What tangible and intangible benefits do you provide to your audiences?*
- **Voice:** *What adjectives would you use to describe your organization/idea?*

Let's try an example from one of my latest projects, restoring funding for outdoor school in Oregon. Outdoor school started in Oregon over sixty years ago. Traditionally it entailed taking sixth-grade students out to the woods, the desert, or the coast for a full week of hands-on science education. The kids lived in cabins with kids from other schools, sat with them at meals, shared chores like cleaning the cabins, and sang a lot. It was all about learning to collaborate and lead by doing. Yet, because of budget cuts, fewer than half of Oregon's kids get to go to outdoor school today. Even those who do attend go for fewer days, and their parents often have to pay for the program. I'm leading a new statewide coalition of community leaders of all kinds to lobby the legislature to create a sustainable funding source for this great program. It is critical that we talk effectively about why this, of all the demands on the state, should be funded.

In developing our message we went through the process of identifying our three Vs. Under each heading and its question we listed what Outdoor School provides.

Values: What core values are central to your organization/idea and connect you to the people you're trying to engage and serve?

- Stewardship of Oregon—its past, present, and future
  - ¤ natural resources and land
  - ¤ ALL our children
  - ¤ our culture and heritage
  - ¤ our economic success
- Applied learning and improved STEM skills
- Civic responsibility
- Collaboration

- ▢ Through coalition
- ▢ Taught through ODS programs
- Health of Oregonians
  - ▢ Physical
  - ▢ Emotional
  - ▢ Psychological
- Self-sufficiency and leadership
- Connection to place and Oregon
- Economic vibrancy
- Equity, bridging the urban-rural divide
- Discovery and inquiry
- Wonder and awe
- Fun

Value: *What tangible and intangible benefits do you provide to your audiences?*

- Transformative educational experiences for students at key life and developmental stages
- Exponential benefits and impacts achieved at very little cost
- Building confidence, self-sufficiency
  - ▢ Social skills, school retention, health, STEM, careers
- Equitable experience that connects all kids to place and one another
  - ▢ Teaching children how to collaborate and work together
- Applied learning that leads to better career and economic opportunities for all Oregonians
- An engaged populace that understands how to be good stewards of our natural resources

Voice: *What adjectives would you use to describe your organization/idea?*

- Balanced
- Inclusive
- Inviting

- Thoughtful/grounded/deliberate
- Informed/knowledgeable
- Inspiring
- Powerful
- Determined/committed ("we're in it for the long haul")
- Urgent, action-oriented
- Resourceful
- Personal

So much good information! So many powerful images! Now comes the hard part: creating a short paragraph you can communicate in only thirty seconds that comprises your offer—that is, how your idea or project relates to values your listener cares about, the benefits or value that your idea or project will deliver, and how you talk about both the problem to be fixed and your solution (your voice, in other words). What kind of elevator speech can I craft out of the above lists corresponding to Values, Value, and Voice? What would *you* say in the thirty seconds that you have that will convey your passion and your talents and why this particular approach or group is the right one? Here's what I came up with:

People from throughout Oregon are coming together to restore outdoor school for all Oregon kids. We call our campaign Outdoor School for All. Outdoor school teaches leadership and collaboration while connecting students with nature and giving them real-world skills and knowledge about Oregon's tremendous natural resources and natural heritage. Currently, fewer than half of our kids get this transformative experience. We need your help to pass legislation this year. Can I count on your support?

Twenty-six seconds.

How did I do? Does this sound like an intriguing idea to you? Do you want to know more? What will you tell yourself, your spouse, your friends, the world? What is *your* offer?

Now, try it with your own idea: Get a piece of paper and write these questions down. You can also do this with others—recommended!—and brainstorm answers to each question. Write them all down, discuss, improve, add on. Then write your own elevator speech.

- **Values:** *What core values are central to your organization/idea and connect you to the people you're trying to engage and serve?*
- **Value:** *What tangible and intangible benefits do you provide to your audiences?*
- **Voice:** *What adjectives would you use to describe your organization/idea?*

ME, A LEADER?

Most people don't usually think of themselves as "leaders." We're just ordinary people doing what we see needs to be done, right? How is that leadership? Don't leaders have to be polished, talkative, knowledgeable (even "know-it-alls"), and somehow different from ordinary folks?

I want you to start thinking of yourself as a leader.

For many people, the first barrier to seeing yourself as a leader is just that, being willing to see yourself as a leader. Let me say this again: the first barrier to seeing yourself as a leader is seeing yourself as a leader.

You will need to forget the stereotypes you might hold about who is a leader, because leaders are people like you. People you run into everyday. What makes these people leaders is that they have figured out how to act on their concerns in ways that make a difference. Not all will be role models, but we can learn so much from each other and help each other. Keeping an eye out for people who inspire you and achieve success is a big part of being a leader yourself.

It won't surprise you that many of these people won't see themselves as "leaders," either. They will tell you, "Oh no, I'm just a simple person trying to fix a little problem." Don't confuse humbleness with being ineffective as a leader. Being humble is about recognizing that we accomplish nothing on our own, that the reward isn't a ticker tape parade—it's the joy and fulfillment of creating a better community or a safer street or a healthier school lunch. Strong leaders are usually quite humble about their roles and accomplishments even if they can be quite fierce when it's time to take a stand.

FROM THE TRENCHES

A "Nerd" from South Central

I met Juan Martinez in Aspen, Colorado, at a fancy conference for environmental leaders. I had gotten a scholarship through the National Geographic Society, and Juan had been invited to speak. He was only twenty-one, from a poor immigrant family who lived in South Central Los Angeles. Yet he had started a national organization of young leaders of color engaged in environmental work called the Natural Leaders Network. I was pretty much in awe, especially as I remembered my comparatively self-indulgent youth filled with seasonal jobs and travel. Juan told his story of growing up in the violent barrio, with the night sky full not of stars but of black LAPD helicopters out chasing gang members. Then he got a break—a teacher told him he could either join the high school ecology club or be expelled. Basically a good kid, if unmotivated, Juan joined the club, willing to suffer the "nerd factor" in order to stay in school and not break his mother's heart. One of the club's projects was growing a garden on the school grounds. He grew peppers and tomatoes. He was so proud to be able to bring them home and make salsa with his mother—using the crops he had grown himself.

The garden kept him in school. His teacher then suggested he apply for a Sierra Club program that took inner-city youth out into the wilderness. Juan was terrified, he told me, and sure a cougar or a bear would eat him. Or that he'd be humiliated because he had never camped, never been out of the barrio before. His first night, the sight of the Milky Way blazing above blew his mind. And changed his life. He went back to his barrio and told everyone he could about how great the natural world was. Then he noticed that there were very few people like him in the environmental movement. Juan was determined to make it so that more young people of color and low income got involved.

This young man—remember, he was only twenty-one when I met him—had already created a group with national reach, with members in most major cities. Here he was, speaking in front of international leaders. But he was just Juan, a kid from South Central, somewhat surprised with all the attention.

Most of the leaders I know don't think of themselves as leaders. I would bet that you also know people who are good at getting things done and who are also reluctant to think of themselves as leaders. Maybe they think they are too old, too young, too uneducated, too different, too ordinary, or too nice to be leaders. Maybe you think of yourself in one of those ways. Even after many years of being in leadership roles, I still have "Who, me?" moments when people turn to me for advice or answers. What right do I have to take on such an important role? Why should people trust me and my ideas? Who am I to presume to speak for anyone else? It's okay. Strong leaders don't have to be perfect or know everything. They do need to be able to say, "How can I help?" and "What else do I need to know?" They also need to have confidence in their leadership skills—enough to counter all those internal "Who, me?" moments and the inevitable external "Why you?" ones. Creating a leadership resume is one way to develop that confidence.

TRY IT NOW #2

Writing Your Leadership Resume

Have you ever thought of writing a resume for leadership? You know how it goes: a resume lists your experiences, skills, and traits that best fit whatever job you are applying for. It may take a little more thinking to tease out what a "job" like "leadership" requires. It's not as easy as typing in "familiar with Word and Excel," or "five years' progressive experience in waiting tables / writing code / project management." Still, leadership experiences abound in life. There are times in our lives where our actions have inspired, motivated, or helped others to reach a goal. That is leadership experience!

- Write down five examples of times you have shown leadership, in any situation. A short paragraph on each will do. In each paragraph include a sentence touching on the following: What happened? What did you do? What skills did you have to use? What traits (such as patience, persistence, curiosity, and empathy) were required?

- Is there one instance specifically connected with the particular issue you are interested in working on, or one relevant to a particular organization you want to work with? If not, do you have a story that shows your ability to inspire and engage?

- Now find a friend or partner. Read them what you wrote. Do they have anything to add? (Especially that stuff you may be too modest to mention.) Ask them to brainstorm with you to come up with five more areas or situations where you showed leadership.

- From this great list of ten examples, can you write a resume that describes the experiences, skills, and traits that make you a leader?

EXHIBIT: LEADERSHIP RESUME

Juanita H. Alvarez

52 Aspen Way

Las Cruces, New Mexico 12001

LEADERSHIP SKILLS AND EXPERIENCE

VOLUNTEER

- Organized march for immigration reform with twenty other regional organizations.
- Provided central communication hub for all press materials regarding the immigration march on September 21, 2012.
- Served on board of Workers Education Center for La Cruz, New Mexico, an organization that provides ESL, health, and legal services for new immigrants.
- Wrote curriculum for ESL classes for Workers Education Center and interviewed and trained new volunteer teachers.
- Established a writing workshop for students struggling with English while a sophomore at the University of New Mexico, Albuquerque. The workshop became a pilot program for other UNM campuses.

PROFESSIONAL

- Trained and managed waitstaff at Taco Loco restaurant.
- Spearheaded unionization effort at Taco Loco restaurant.
- Initiated free ESL workshops for non-English-speaking staff at Taco Loco restaurant.
- Negotiated with local community organizations to secure a space for Taco Loco ESL workshops.
- Wrote and disseminated flyers about immigrant worker rights at local restaurants in Albuquerque.

WARNING! EGO AHEAD!

Unfortunately, there are some self-styled leaders who take all the credit for the success of group efforts or act as if no one could accomplish anything without them. Playing the stereotypical "leader," with too little humility, is a short-lived strategy. What these people eventually discover is that they are alone when they most need supporters. They get frustrated when people don't see the truth as they see it. They too often end up bitter, and they quit because the world hasn't bent to their vision. Be careful not to fall prey to the big-ego model of leadership. Success, in the long run—remember what evolution teaches us—is a community thing.

FINDING YOUR PLACE IN THE COMMUNITY ECOSYSTEM

Sometimes, people will see you as a leader by virtue of external qualities—or the opposite may happen. For example, I am a white middle-class male who was lucky enough to get a great public education. There are a lot of doors open to me. I can walk into a boardroom or a city council chamber without feeling out of place. No one asks me to justify my presence or questions my right to my opinions or my right to speak them—because of my status as a white middle-class male. I fit in, and I am often perceived as a leader in some groups because of what I am, not necessarily because of my great ideas or fancy speech. Even if my ideas weren't always mainstream, I was. This is a tremendous advantage that I didn't even realize I had until some strong leaders pointed it out to me.

It took me some time, and work, to understand the very real advantages I had as a white middle-class male. I came to realize that what I took as givens—access and respect—were things many people in my community didn't have. Acknowledging my privileged status helped me build alliances across race and class lines. My new allies taught me how white privilege not only helped me but also, paradoxically, limited what I could accomplish. Being educated, white, and middle class comes with its own restrictive stereotypes about leadership that made me doubt my capabilities and lowered my expectations of what I could hope to achieve—even as my white privilege opened doors! Let me explain.

Power in our society is communicated in many ways: what clothes you wear, the school you attended, what clubs you belong to, who you meet for drinks. Even being a white man, I was still trained to defer to others. For example, if someone in a Brooks Brothers suit started expounding in an upper-crust accent, referring to their Harvard education and exotic vacations, I, like many others, unconsciously deferred to them and their opinions. They, in turn, expected this deference. Their very expectation of power gives them power.

My allies helped me realize that I was unconsciously using the same strategies to try to get my way—using my whiteness and education as means to power. When I was working with low-income and minority communities, this blew up in my face. Entitlement shows to others, even it you can't see it. It really turns people off. Now, no one can change the color of their skin or undo their education, nor would I want them to. I will never know what it is like to have grown up black or poor or gone to bad schools. But, by becoming conscious of how race and class affect our communities and our relations, I can better recognize the insights, passions, and ideas that everyone has. And these insights, passions, and ideas can be very powerful—if people are able and willing to share them with you. Recognizing your own privilege, whatever the source, is the first step in opening up the dialogue and building the trusting relationships necessary to create powerful alliances and friendships across social barriers.

Next, we will see how to overcome our differences of circumstances and origins to build trust and grow leaders.

RECOGNIZE LEADERS IN UNEXPECTED PLACES

Leaders show up in some of the most unexpected places, and they can be the most unexpected people. Just as you need to learn your place in the community ecosystem, you need to drop your preconceptions about where leaders will appear in that ecosystem.

FROM THE TRENCHES

How One Woman Busted My Preconceived Notions and Taught Me More Than Twenty Years of Schooling

Sylvia Evans schooled me in finding leaders in unexpected places. I met Sylvia, an African American single mother of two, when she agreed to host a transportation planning workshop in her home. She lives in a public housing complex in inner-city Portland. She proudly told me she lived where she did because she was an environmentalist!

I fancied myself a great bike-riding environmentalist (while owning two cars and a three-bedroom home). Sylvia consciously chose to live near transit, in a neighborhood with sidewalks, where her children could walk to school because she knew that car ownership and use is one of the major causes of our most critical environmental problems, from climate change to rising obesity rates to accidental death and injury. She refused to limit herself and her concerns to my preconceptions of what her problems should be. Or what values motivated her to action.

She volunteered to host a workshop for us because she knew that this was the only way her community would be heard. She wanted us to hear her community's ideas, concerns, and perspectives. She wanted us to hear, in their own words, her neighbors' concerns about air pollution, safer streets, and better bus service. Sylvia's leadership helped redefine transportation in Portland by adding a crucial, missing perspective—that of low-income, minority residents. Because most transportation planners and policy makers are middle class and white, we had been talking mostly to white middle-class audiences, reflecting again the unconscious biases that come with being in a privileged position in society.

Sylvia showed me that a leader doesn't need an Ivy League education, a fancy job title, or a confident strut. *She showed me that leaders are those who take on responsibility for their communities.*

The most effective leaders, what I call strong leaders, are very intentional about how they approach leadership. They don't care who gets credit for results or for the group's or team's success. Strong leaders don't just punch the clock. They are always thinking about how they can be better leaders so they can get more done. By thinking of yourself *as a leader*, you will be able to connect and contribute more deeply to the work and your community, whatever role you currently have. Not everyone serves as executive director or leads the parade, but all of us can set priorities, speak the truth, and provide emotional support to others when they need it. We can all insist that all voices be heard and respected. This is what strong leaders do.

ARE YOU HOUSEBROKEN? DON'T BE!

The sad fact is that few of us get the encouragement and training we need to be leaders. For most of our school years, we are told to sit still and listen. We are told that "real" leaders look, talk, and dress differently from us. We are told that when we stand up for what we think is right, we are troublemakers or dreamers who expect too much. (Look at who is telling you this—those who benefit from, or are just too comfortable with, the ways things are.) Mocking and patronizing people who are different makes it easy to dismiss ideas that challenge the status quo. How frustrating this can be to the well-meaning person trying to make a difference in their community!

As Sylvia taught me—and she was one of my many teachers—our own prejudices can be the biggest obstacle we need to overcome to be strong leaders. In the section "Open Heart, Open Mind" (in chapter two), we will explore further how you can tap into the power of the whole community's diverse perspectives and experiences to overcome social conditioning to accept things the way they are.

INSIDER VERSUS OUTSIDER

When I met Sylvia, I had been in elected office for two years. I had struggled to figure out how I could continue my work to make change while in a very public position that also required me to work on stuff I frankly didn't care that much about. It was a bit of a crisis for me: I had been a community activist for so long . . . Could I keep my street cred as an effective leader for social change if I had—gulp—an office and a secretary and oversaw a half-billion-dollar enterprise?

Some people think that you can't be an activist, advocate, or leader if you work for "The Man." That if you work for government or a corporation, there is no way you can keep your credibility as someone working for a better world. Even though this kind of thinking is wrong on numerous levels, you will run into it a lot in activist circles. Some people associate activism with living as an ascetic, denying yourself the world's pleasures, including time with friends and family. Many of my fellow classmates at graduate school had worked for one of the many public interest research groups founded by the arch-ascetic/activist Ralph Nader. They told stories of working long hours canvassing door-to-door and then being berated by their crew leaders for not staying around for a group pizza party, unpaid, when they wanted to go home to their families.

Some activists, along with many journalists, believe that all governments and corporations are engaged in conspiracies to commit crimes against people and nature. They just need to be uncovered! You and I know there are plenty of examples of malfeasance and corruption in these institutions, but when passionate and committed people avoid working for them, the only ones left on the inside of these powerful institutions will be those in it for personal gain or ideological ends. Political campaigns to demonize government in all its forms have scared many good people away from considering running for office or having public service careers. I know many people who would be great elected officials, but I can't get them to consider running for office because they are cynical, suspicious, or worried about having their personal lives torn apart by malicious scrutiny. This destructive depiction of public servants as greedy or incompetent certainly hasn't stopped groups that defame public service from running candidates or appointing their cronies to high office!

PUBLIC SERVICE

Being on the inside certainly presents new challenges to an activist or community leader. Let me go over a few I faced and how I figured out how to deal with them and still be an effective activist. After taking office, I soon found a large and diverse community of interests knocking on my door with their agendas and demands. I struggled to balance my personal agenda with outside as well as internal demands for attention and leadership. One thing I did was ask my ex-colleagues in community organizations to keep up the pressure on me and my agency. I told them that their "friends" in office constantly face pressure from many interest groups to meet their demands. By continuing their advocacy with me, I was able to honestly declare that my positions were based on what my community wanted.

Another successful strategy I discovered was making personal connections with public employees. This became an important part of my being effective as a leader, whether it was when I was an activist trying to get my ideas heard or as their boss. I discovered that most public employees are very proud of their work and happy to answer my questions—if I approached them as a fellow citizen who cared about their community. In time, as we grew to trust and respect each other (even if we disagreed), they would let me know about opportunities to influence policies that would help further my goals.

I first heard the term *guerrilla bureaucrat* from Michael Carr, a Texas bicycle advocate brought to Portland for a citizens' summit on transportation. More than twenty years later, I still remember him telling the audience about this idea during a humorous description of his Four Laws of Bureaucracy, based on Newton's laws of motion. You may remember these from your middle school science class: one was "A bureaucrat at rest tends to stay at rest unless acted upon by an outside force," to quote Carr, who recommended, tongue in cheek, a two-by-four as a good outside force. A guerrilla bureaucrat is someone who works for a government agency and is sympathetic with your cause. A guerilla bureaucrat is willing to use their insider knowledge to make sure that the community is aware of actions and opportunities that can affect them. Those actions and opportunities may not be communicated very well by their agency, particularly if the agency's leaders fear controversy or complicated decision-making. As you probably have discovered in your life, the community often only realizes something is happening when the bulldozers show up. The important decisions had been made long before, sometimes years in advance. Having a friend on the inside is incredibly valuable as they can direct you to key decision points as well as help you understand the consequences of different choices.

I valued my guerrilla bureaucrats and treated them well. Always thanking them, always confirming the information they gave me through other sources so they wouldn't run afoul of their bosses (e.g., going to the agency websites and digging for hidden announcements), and respecting them for the good work they do.

I'm sure you have friends who have chosen public service careers. This is an honorable choice and a great way to contribute to society while making a living. If you have been effective in your community making change happen, you may find yourself being asked to join the very agency you've been pushing to change. Or, like me, you might be asked to run for office. Don't shy away from the chance! Being on the inside can be a great way to move your agenda forward and to help your community achieve their goals.

HARNESSING BUSINESS SAVVY FOR CHANGE

People in business need a lot of different skills to be successful, from accounting to personnel management to legal know-how. Community organizations can benefit from their expertise, expertise you may not have or be able to afford. Community groups often recruit businesspeople to serve on their boards to access their skills and drive. I've asked my board's "legal guy" for advice not just on how to keep in compliance with the IRS but also for legal strategies that we might use to force a recalcitrant agency to respond to our demands. In fact, this is how my underfunded, mostly volunteer bicycling advocacy group ended up successfully suing the City of Portland. (Using an all-volunteer legal team, we won a precedent-setting case that enforced an old and ignored state law requiring all Oregon governments to take into account the safety of people walking and cycling by installing bike lanes and sidewalks as part of all road projects.)

All sorts of people will join your group because they care about the issues. Who knows, your local banker might also be a big fan of a particular activity or have a family history that connects them to your issue. Make it a point to find out what your members or fellow volunteers do for work, what motivates them, and what other causes they volunteer for in the community. It was surprising and exciting when I saw the names of prominent businesspeople start showing up on our mailing lists. Who knew that they loved riding bicycles! I called them and asked if they could help us pitch our ideas to local business groups—their people—such as chambers of commerce. It's much easier to pitch your idea to a group when one of their own introduces and advocates for it first!

There are many opportunities in the private sector to be an activist, as well. A growing number of companies recognize that they have a greater role to play in society than just making money. One way a company demonstrates this commitment is to incorporate as what is known as a B Corporation. Social responsibility is actually written into the company's articles of incorporation along with the standard fiduciary duty to their stockholders. Other companies often pay for their employees to volunteer in their community or match employee donations to local organizations. You may be able to help incorporate sustainability into your business practices (it will save money in the long run!) or to get conversations going about diversity and inclusion in the workplace. Ask your human resources person about how your company supports involvement in your community.

FROM THE TRENCHES

Businesses Get a Boost from Activism (and Activism Gets a Boost from Business!)

The Community Cycling Center began in Portland in the early 1990s, based in a low-income, mostly minority community. The CCC teaches people how to maintain their bicycles themselves, introduces them to the benefits of cycling, and even subsidizes bicycle purchases for low-income workers and their children. They also offer summer camps for kids to give them, and their parents, confidence in their cycling skills, especially around traffic. But their signature activity is their Holiday Bike Drive. With donated bikes, and hundreds of volunteers working to spruce them up, the CCC partners with local social service agencies to identify families who can't afford to buy their kids a bike. A gift of a new bike! You can just imagine the smiles on the kids' faces when a volunteer fits them out with a helmet and they get to pick out their bike from hundreds on the floor! A new company moving to the Portland area recently sought out the CCC as a partner. The company was looking to establish a bigger presence in the community as part of its business development strategy. They saw the Holiday Bike Drive as a great way to get noticed; they became a major sponsor and gave the largest single donation the CCC had ever received.

MOVING OUT OF YOUR COMFORT ZONE

Those with power protect their power. They utilize barriers of class, education, family connections, and race. It can be a wonder that so many people without the advantages of privilege or access become strong leaders for social change. How did people like Cesar Chavez, Ron Dellums, and Elizabeth Norton overcome these daunting obstacles? By understanding what it really means to be a leader, starting with thinking that they can lead and reaching out to others who shared their dreams for a better world even if they looked different, sounded different, or offered different answers.

Leadership will mean talking to people different from you, who might seem to have quite different values and ideas about what is best for the community. Hanging out with, sitting at the same table as, and oftentimes arguing with people unlike you can be intimidating. Sometimes our reaction to going beyond our comfort zone is giving in too easily or, conversely, thinking it's too hard, not worth the effort. So caught up in seeing things in an us-and-them way, we don't see mutually beneficial solutions. Successful leaders avoid getting bogged down by social stereotypes and expectations. Successful leaders are clear about their goals. Successful leaders connect all their actions, attitudes, and expectations to the outcomes they want to achieve. It's not about you. It's not about them. It's about the community that we hope to live in. Its about this place that we care enough about to get involved in shaping its future.

CHAPTER I BLUEPRINT FOR CHANGE

In this chapter you learned how to identify what motivates you to work for change and how to:

- Take those first steps to transform your passion for a cause into action.
- Share your passion with a succinct thirty-second "Elevator Speech."
- Think of yourself as a leader and create your own "leadership resume."
- Find your place within the community ecosystem—starting with recognizing your place of privilege and power.
- Tap the power of leaders in your community—they come in all shapes, colors, and sizes.
- Reconcile your role as a business or government insider with your role as an activist.

CHAPTER 2

PUTTING THE "ACT" IN *ACTIVIST*: PREPARING TO LEAD

"Power isn't control at all—power is strength, and giving
that strength to others. A leader isn't someone who forces
others to make him stronger; a leader is someone willing to
give his strength to others that they may have the strength
to stand on their own."
—*Beth Revis*, Across the Universe

What I love most about becoming involved in something new are the friendships I make with people I would probably never had met in my "normal," day-to-day life. Getting invited to a powwow at the Native American Youth and Family Center in northeast Portland to watch the dancers, eat fry bread, and talk with young people proudly sporting their buckskins and feathers about their plans for college . . . Or trying to dance salsa with the woman from Colombia at the Educate Ya Gala and laughing along with her at my swivel-less hips. At the break (at last!) we talk about the work she does with young immigrant women trying to help their kids succeed in schools with little resources for non-English speakers. The learning and camaraderie that come from working with others are what fuel me when the work is more difficult. Like when I'm calling people to ask them for money for a new cause or when I prepare for a difficult negotiation.

Maybe you feel the same way. My hope and commitment get reignited by the passion and energy of people working to change the world. A few years ago, I met a young woman, a sixteen-year-old high school student from Eugene, who was suing the state of Oregon for failing to protect her generation (and the earth) from the impacts of global warming. There is an ancient legal doctrine called "the public trust" that holds that the government has a duty to protect the essential ingredients of life—clean air, clean water, free passage. Hers is one of many such lawsuits around the country, each with a young person as plaintiff seeking to protect their future by forcing real action from governments today to reduce carbon emissions. These young people are so articulate, so purposeful! How can I not be inspired and goaded into doing more myself?

All is not happiness and light, though. When you seek to change the world, and take on a leadership role, you will inevitably find yourself in conflict with others— sometimes even with your loved ones and even yourself! Your friends and family may feel shortchanged, competing for your time and attention. You may feel unappreciated and resentful when others fail to support your efforts and ideas. You will work hard and despair at how little impact you seem to be having on the problem. You will be angry when people disparage you and tell lies about you. You will be hurt when your best intentions are misinterpreted.

In Japan they have a saying: "The nail that sticks up gets hammered down." I've been that nail and I've known that hammer, and you may have, too.

In my forty years of activism, sometimes I've been fooled, disappointed, frustrated, and even betrayed. Despite the potential for heartache, there is just so much work needing to be done to make the world a better place. Our communities need us to stand up and take risks. The flip side is that most of the time it is so rewarding and also fun to work with others on a good cause (see above about salsa dancing and fry bread!). In order to flourish as a leader, you should anticipate disappointment.

There are steps you can take to prepare yourself so you can maintain your enthusiasm and commitment even when things get tough. Sometimes you will fail. Others may fail you. You will also be successful. And be astounded by the love and support you get.

FINDING MEANING AND PURPOSE IN YOUR LIFE

As long as humans have told stories and kept histories, we've told tales about people facing and overcoming difficulties. Fables like the Tortoise and the Hare or Little Red Riding Hood show how pluck, perserverance, and perspective allow even the weak and the slow to prevail. We've also debated right and wrong, rights and responsibilities, liberty and duty. In Greece more than two thousand years ago, philosophers fiercely debated what it meant to live a "good life." In particular, they argued about the proper balance between one's duty to one's community and individual freedom. Fundamentally these were debates about what it means to be a citizen—an active member of a community. They asked questions such as: What were the rights of the individual? What did the individual owe to their tribe or clan? What did the powerful owe the weak? We know about these debates because some were written down and survived through the centuries, copied and translated by later writers because these are always relevant topics. The arguments of ancient Greek philosophers such as Plato and Aristotle on ethics and the duty of the individual to society still underlie political discussions in the European-influenced world, just as the writings of Confucius on duty and purpose still influence Asian political thought today.

In ancient Greece, the Stoics were one of the most influential philosophical schools. In about 300 BC, philosophers of the Stoic school argued that the only reliable measure of truth and reality is our own experience. That is, all we can really know for sure is how the world affects us personally and how we respond, in our own feelings and through our actions, to the world. Philosophical debates in those days could get fierce, and the Stoics were eventually forced out of Athens and their works mostly destroyed. Some Stoics were even killed for their views because their championing of the individual over the state was seen as treasonous. The result is that much of surviving Greek writing about Stoicism consists of satires, written by their enemies. In these versions, Stoics were portrayed as lacking normal human emotions (think Spock of the original *Star Trek* television series) or as anarchists, because they rejected any authority outside of one's own experience and conscience.

Although very little original Stoic writing survived, many in the ancient world continued to practice and write about this approach to life's difficult questions. The Roman emperor Marcus Aurelius (AD 121–180) is one of the most famous followers of Stoicism. He wrote extensively on its practice and philosophy. His collected letters are surprisingly modern in their language and tone, still relevant to issues we deal with today, despite being written almost two thousand years ago. In them he wrestles with critical questions such as:

- How should we respond to inevitable setbacks and failures?
- Is there something more than animal instinct or blind faith to rely on for conducting our lives in authentic and positive ways?
- What is the proper balance between the rights of each person versus the duty of the individual to the state or broader community?

I discovered Stoic philosophy by chance one night when I attended a live taping of the public radio show *Philosophy Talk*. The guest that night was Dr. William Irvine of Ohio's Wright State University. He himself had rediscovered the Stoics in middle age. Although he claimed he was not a religious person, as a younger man he had been drawn to the clear-eyed appraisal of life that Zen Buddhism espoused. Yet Dr. Irvine wasn't entirely comfortable with Eastern philosophy, he told the audience that night, because of how unfamiliar the Asian perspective was to his Western mind. By chance, he had picked up a copy of Marcus Aurelius's writings, which he had studied briefly as an undergraduate. In those pages, he rediscovered someone who wrestled with the issues he was struggling with, such as trying to find meaning in mortality, in a reversal of fortunes, or in the death of loved ones. And all of it was written in an accessible, familiar manner.

What does Aurelius say that struck Dr. Irvine so? He reminds us that life *is* tough. And tragic. Simply because we will die. No way around it. Aurelius tells us that we can still be effective and happy if we concern ourselves with those things we have control over and accept that there are many things we don't have any control over whatsoever. Stoics thought it a waste of energy and time to grieve too much or to harbor resentment or jealousy—or even to rejoice too much. (This is the source of the myth that a stoic person doesn't smile or cry. Stiff upper lip and all that. Grief and joy are part of human life. The trick is not to let strong emotions rule your reason or your life.) Just like the Buddhists and people following other similar traditions, the Stoics developed exercises of self-reflection and meditation to cultivate and retain this perspective. Like Dr. Irvine, I found the Stoic perspective and exercises very helpful, and I hope you will, too.

FROM THE TRENCHES

Stoic Thought for Activists

See life as it is. There is no need for elaborate theologies or ideologies to give life meaning. KBOO (90.7 FM) is an institution in Portland. For over forty years, this nonprofit radio station has been a place where anyone and everyone can get their ideas or their music out to the community. 90.7 FM is where I got exposed to rap and hip-hop for the first time, along with Latino and Native concerns, lesbian politics, and the voices of people in prison. Alan Bailey was station director for many years, raising money, fighting federal regulators when volunteer DJs crossed FCC boundaries, and trying to get a very diverse and passionate group of people working together and respecting their differences. He was only fifty years old when he was diagnosed with cancer. He kept working through treatments, and we were thrilled when he announced he was in remission. Then he was diagnosed with MS. Then his cancer returned. I asked him how he kept at it, with all the challenges and indignities of two debilitating and terminal diseases. He told me that he saw no other choice. He'd dedicated his life to KBOO and its vibrant community, so why should he stop just because he was dying? Weren't we all?

Your experience of life is the truest guide to reality. Everyday we are told by someone—whether an activist blogger, the media, a preacher, or a politician—that others are evil, dangerous, or anti-whatever-it-is-at-the-moment. Recently I asked a forest industry organization to help pay for an outreach effort to gain support for funding outdoor education in Oregon. The board included representatives of some of the most conservative businesses in Oregon, including the local Koch Brothers representative. She chaired the group! All my liberal alarms went off. As I listened to them talk about their desire to have Oregonians, especially urban dwellers, understand how forestry works, the struggle of hardworking, rural people to support their families, and their industry's efforts to become more sustainable, I realized that we shared a good deal. We all wanted good jobs, clean water, and opportunities for people to know more about and enjoy nature. My personal experience, hearing what they feared and aspired to, was a truer guide than anything I had read or heard. I was able to speak to them about how my project, getting kids out into nature to appreciate it and understand our dependence and use of natural resources, connected to their concerns. I got their support and funding.

A good life is achieved by doing even mundane things well. Duty is its own reward. My wife, Lydia, taught in Portland's inner-city schools for almost thirty years. Each year, a new wave of youngsters would enter her classroom door, bringing with them both their excitement and their challenges. Many came from households with no parents, with fathers in prison, or with mothers on the streets. Lydia tied their shoes, held their hands, looked them in the eye, and told them, "You wouldn't want Jonathan to hit you, so how do you think he feels when you hit him?" Day in, day out. For decades the same songs, the same skinned knees, the same feeling of frustration when she knew a child was damaged and there was only so much she could do. But she loved her work. Even in retirement she is thinking about children all the time, studying the latest research and volunteering at low-income day care centers. It wasn't about winning or a big paycheck. Lydia knew she was doing good, even while making the thousandth batch of Play-Doh she had made in her life.

I hope you will find examining your life's choices in an intentional way as useful and enlightening as I have found this practice. Self-reflection prepares you for both activism and leadership. It is more than a way to feel calm in a decidedly upsetting world. It has given me a structure on which to build purposeful engagement with others and help me keep to a clear path for action. It also gives me a better idea of my civic duty—a useful and unfortunately underused term—and also the limits of my responsibility, helping me avoid feelings of guilt and inadequacy that are counterproductive and unnecessary, to boot. Stoic philosophy really resonates with me. Do you have a framework that helps you make sense of life?

TRY IT NOW #3

Think of the Worst First

Try out this simple Stoic exercise: Marcus Aurelius described it two thousand years ago, and Dr. Irvine expanded on it in his work. It really stuck with me, and it helps me make sense of life when things get crazy.

On waking in the morning, take five minutes to contemplate the worst thing that could happen to you today. Most of us would agree that the death of a person close to us would be about the most devastating thing we can imagine. We would experience profound grief, overwhelming feelings of loss, and an inability to figure out what to do next. Right? Even as a thought experiment, thinking about losing my wife or sons is pretty overwhelming! Now, reflect on the fact that while this horrible thing will happen someday, it isn't likely to happen today. Now, think about the challenges and concerns you will face in the day ahead, the ones that made it hard to sleep last night; in comparison to this calamity, everything else is quite manageable. A setback at work, a flat tire, an unfavorable vote. What are these compared to real tragedy? Hardly worth worrying about!

Contrary to popular portrayals of Stoicism, Stoics don't undervalue emotions like grief and love. It is only natural to feel hurt and sadness when something goes wrong. Likewise to get overexcited when things go well! Letting emotions such as hurt and fear and even jubilation overcome us makes us less able to act effectively, sometimes just when action is most necessary. By choosing not to "take life personally" we can better understand the issues and manage our relationships with others.

Next time you feel as if you are being attacked or failing, try asking yourself, "Why did they?" or "Why did this happen?" rather than "How could they?" or "How did this happen to me?" This will shift your focus from your feelings of hurt or disappointment—recognizing that what you control is your reaction to events rather than the events themselves—enabling you to focus on finding strategies that can change behaviors and outcomes.

Recent scientific studies confirm the wisdom of this approach. In studies of how the brain operates when people worry, scientists found that worrying actually *reduces the blood flow to the cerebral cortex*—the part of the brain where high-level reasoning takes place. It also leads to about a fifteen-point drop in IQ! There you go! Proof that we are our own worst enemy when we let emotions overwhelm our ability to act. Practicing self-reflection with exercises like the one above when you aren't in the midst of a crisis will help you immensely when things get difficult, which they will. Hey, that's life, as Marcus Aurelius would say!

So, what about getting excited when we win? What's wrong with that?

There are two dangers in expressing even positive emotions too much. It is very easy for others to experience your joy in succeeding—or "winning"—as prideful boasting, or an expression of superiority, or of taking credit personally. Getting carried away with success makes it easy to forget that true progress always results from group effort. It can also blind us to common interests that exist between us as people, even if today we are arrayed on opposing sides of an issue. Leaders who forget this too often finds themselves alone.

Find other useful Stoic exercises at: http://blogs.exeter.ac.uk/stoicismtoday.

MANAGING CHANGE IN YOUR LIFE

Sometimes you choose change and sometimes change chooses you.

I had lost a hard-fought and bitter election campaign. I had been in office for ten years and was excited about the future. I was making plans for a whole new set of initiatives. On election night everything changed. All my plans and ideas were suddenly irrelevant. I felt irrelevant and adrift. I called up a man I had met during my campaign and who had impressed me with his insights and success in life. Don Washburn had been a CEO of some major firms, including a national airline. He was now settled in Portland, volunteering and serving on a few corporate boards. I called him up out of the blue to get his advice on dealing with this unexpected change in my life. He gave me this advice: *get ready for serendipity*. *Serendipity* is such a great word! It means a happy accident, a pleasant surprise, or more specifically, *finding something good or useful while not intentionally searching for it*. What happens when you take a random turn when walking in an unfamiliar city. Every new sight is a revelation!

So what does serendipity have to do with losing an election, with looking for work? Don pointed out to me the importance of knowing yourself well before you start looking for what's next. If you know what really motivates you, what you are passionate about, when opportunities appear you will be better able to tell if they are right for you. In addition to making the hunt for fulfilling work or volunteer positions more strategic, being clear about your values and passions will allow you to take advantage of opportunities that appear unexpectedly—that is, serendipitously. The key thing he stressed to me, over and over, is that change is something you can and should prepare for. Don suggested this exercise to me and I urge you to try it, too.

TRY IT NOW #4

Put Your Life in a Letter

Write a letter to your family (or to a trusted friend). You can send your letter or not, but write it as if you are going to send it. Take it seriously. Tell this person about your life:

- What were the choices that really affected your life?
- Why did you make those particular choices?
- What specifically moved you, stirred your passions, and shaped your life?
- My passion was nature. I loved tromping through the woods, overturning rocks to find bugs and salamanders, climbing trees, and fishing. These interests led me to apply for summer jobs with the Forest Service and to study biology in college. Further on in life, I volunteered to plant trees with Friends of Trees and worked to promote recycling and bicycling, and to reduce impacts on our society from climate change.

In your letter, it is critical, very critical, to tell the *why* rather than the what of your life:

- Do you believe in a god? How does your faith affect your ideas about duty, authority, and responsibility?
- Do you believe there is a right way to live? What does this look like?
- Would you recommend this way of life to others?
- How did you decide to work in your chosen career?
- If you went to college, why did you study what you studied?
- Looking back over your life, were there things you would have avoided or choices you would have made differently?

- Looking forward, how might these insights affect how you evaluate choices that come your way?

This exercise helped me better understand who I was and how I got that way. I found it to be a lot of fun—mine went to twelve pages! Longest letter I've ever written! We don't often have the chance or take the time to explain our choices, even to ourselves. Writing this letter is a way to get you thinking about what motivates and excites you so you are ready when serendipity brings you opportunities or life brings you unexpected changes!

Interesting job opening? An invitation to become a board member of a community organization? Someone asking you to run for office? Should you do it? This letter will help you know if this opportunity is right for you.

LEADERS AREN'T LONERS: GETTING HELP

All projects are easier with help. Building a house, digging a garden, even making dinner is always easier if you have someone to answer questions, demonstrate the proper technique, or help you lift that heavy cast-iron pot.

Some of us are fortunate to have a spouse or a group of friends we confide in regularly. These people may have enough life experience and wisdom so that their advice is all you need. Yet they also know one side of you very well and don't know what else burns inside you. I feel very lucky that I can always talk things over with my spouse, but we usually focus on immediate decisions—what to have for dinner—or specific subjects—getting the kids to do their homework.

Other people can be a great source of new ideas and strategies to help you turn your passion into your life's work and to be more successful, as well. Here's my story about how I finally figured out how to ask for help—in a more intentional way— when I found myself in a new role and dealing with new and unfamiliar challenges.

FROM THE TRENCHES

How I Got Game

Oregon, among its many quirks, has the only directly elected regional government in the country. This government, called Metro, is in charge of regional planning and services for a metropolitan region that includes twenty-five cities, including the state's largest, Portland. Along with running a zoo, a convention center, a park system, and the disposal of a million tons of solid waste every year, Metro also oversees regional transportation investments and urban planning. This oversight role creates incredible opportunities to influence policy affecting almost two million people. In the 1990s, I helped bring together a new coalition of community-based organizations with the mission of using Metro's power to advance social and environmental sustainability throughout the Portland metropolitan region: the Coalition for a Livable Future. Through this process, I learned about Metro and became more and more excited about its potential to make significant change happen. Subsequently, I ran for a seat on the Metro Council, defeating a three-term incumbent.

I won! I was so thrilled to have a chance to oversee this big, important agency, with a half-billion-dollar annual operating budget and thousands of employees. I was going to really make things happen! I took my responsibilities very seriously, reading every staff report (and sending them back to be rewritten, with typos circled and grammar corrected, thank you very much). I would spend hours researching and asking questions, trying to understand each and every issue coming before the council. I met with staff. I attended just about every community gathering I was invited to. Spoiler alert! I was spending so many hours trying to be and do everything that I was making very little progress on the things I had vowed to accomplish if elected: climate change, affordable housing, building a bicycle-friendly region. Six months into the job, I was tired, unhappy, and not sure what I was accomplishing there. Going to meetings and working sixty-plus hours a week wasn't working with two school-age kids at home and a spouse with her own stressful job.

What was I doing wrong? I had twenty years' experience as an activist as well as a graduate degree in nonprofit management. I couldn't even get through the daily pile of paperwork! I finally reached out for help. I needed someone who knew the ropes of elected office. Someone who had been effective. I wanted to know their secrets.

Bev Stein was former chair of the Multnomah County Commission. I had met her years before while lobbying as an activist. She was a warm and caring person, plus she supported my activist efforts. I thought, "Here's someone who was very successful in a much more stressful job" (the county chair is also the CEO of the county). She was now a national consultant but still living in town, so I gave her a call. She agreed to be my coach at a "hometown" rate of half her usual price. I told her about how overwhelmed I felt and my frustration at not getting the things done I wanted to do. She started out by having me write out my goals for my time in office, something I hadn't done before. She asked me to tell her why I ran for office in the first place. She asked me what my passions were. (See a pattern here?) Her questions helped me understand my role as an elected official better, as well as come up with ways to be conscientious without losing the balance of work, family, and fun.

She helped me understand what my job was and how to do it more effectively. It wasn't my job to proofread every piece of paper produced by agency staff (the stack could reach a foot high every day). My role as leader was to focus on policy and the budgets that put that policy into action, not grammar. She counseled me to spend time getting to know my fellow councilors better, to get out of my office and spend time with them outside of formal meetings. Having a drink, going to lunch, I got to know them as people. This helped me understand their motivations and interests, and vice versa. Trust developed. I discovered I could share with the other councilors some of the responsibility of understanding the various areas Metro operated in. What a relief this was! Bev's advice allowed me to identify and focus on my primary concerns. I took this advice further and built strong relationships with other leaders—including other elected officials and business and community leaders. I also had more time to talk with constituents and hear their ideas. I could develop the personal connections I needed to win support for new approaches to the many challenges all large metropolitan areas face. After six months of meeting bimonthly, Bev told me that she was finished with me. I had learned the skills that I needed to manage a diverse and complex information flow. I had established relationships with key partners on the council and outside the agency based on trust and open communication. I had learned to balance the demands of work and community with the needs of my family and myself. I was on my way to being a successful leader as an elected official!

Having a coach like Bev was a lifesaver for me. So, how do you go about getting a coach for yourself? Your organization may have a budget for training, and you can hire a certified life coach or, as in my case, pay someone who has been successful in a similar situation. Type life coach into your search engine and you will be amazed at how many "life coaches" are out there.

The challenge, just like finding a good plumber or carpenter, is finding the one who will understand what you need and give you useful guidance. The best way to do this is to ask others in similar positions to yours: Have you worked with a coach? What were your experiences? Would you recommend a particular person? Anyone certified as a coach will have references you should check. In doing so you may find others who are facing similar challenges with whom you can share experiences. This can be as simple as having lunch regularly, with an agenda, to go over each other's current difficulties and discoveries about how to do the work better. It's not often we can get away from the "what" of our work to think critically about the "why" and the "how." Give it a try. Great insights come from taking the time to look at your work from a new perspective.

FROM THE TRENCHES

Creating Your Community Brain Trust

Coaching was really helpful to me in understanding how to be more effective with my time, but it wasn't enough. I still needed help in developing my ideas and strategies, as well as help in actually getting them implemented. I needed *other people's* insights and connections to help me grow my ideas, develop new ones, and make them happen. With Bev's urging and help, I called up some people I had met through my community involvement and asked them if they would help me out. People who cared for me personally, as well as about the issues I cared for. One was my successor as director of the Bicycle Transportation Alliance. Another was a consultant on transportation and community engagement (and occasional whisky-drinking partner). One taught my son in third grade and got me involved in the startup of an alternative middle school. Another was head of a local business association in my district who had impressed me with his insights and solution-oriented approach. Each brought a different perspective and set of skills, but all shared a deep commitment to improving this place they called home.

In all, I recruited six people. They met with me twice a year for a half day of brainstorming and debate around questions like these: What key issues are coming up in the next year? How is my effort to reform regional transportation policy or establish affordable housing strategies going? Who could I get on my side and what would move them? How am I going to do that? What are my next steps?

What I got out of these sessions were lists of ideas, some great camaraderie, and a work plan for the next six months. I also got some tough love—to keep me focused on the important stuff—and inspiration, too. All this for a plate of cookies and some coffee if it was morning or a six-pack of beer, wine, and crackers if it was afternoon. As a bonus, they let me know that I could pick up the phone anytime and call when I had a question, needed their advice, or was looking for a way to influence a key person or connect with a key community. They shared in the excitement of being part of a focused, effective group.

I wish I had learned earlier about the value of getting a bunch of good, smart people together to help me sort my priorities as well as better understand my strengths and weaknesses. But it's never too late to ask for a hand. Here's how you can go about building your team:

1. Make a list of the skills and knowledge *you* would love to have.

2. Think of people you've worked with in your community. Make a list of those who've impressed you with their thoughtfulness, insight, and compassion.

3. Sort your list by a few broad categories. You might want someone with knowledge of a specific issue, say, an expert on education or water policy. You will probably want someone who is good at relationships—you can tell they have this skill because when you see them with others, there is a certain glow. Maybe someone who has run a campaign or who lobbies in the legislature would be helpful.

4. Consider this, as well: Are these people you like? Do they like each other? To look at it another way, are these people you think would be fun to have over for dinner? You will be exposing yourself, your fears, and your hopes, and they probably will, as well. You want people to be comfortable being open with each other. You want this to be a fun experience, even if it is very serious.

5. Does this group represent your community? One danger of only inviting your friends is that you will only get echoes of your own perspective or miss out on a critical community issue affecting people outside your current circle.

6. Provide stuff to eat and drink. Food is the first step in community building. It doesn't have to be fancy, and there doesn't have to be a lot of it.

7. Be serious. Have an agenda, flip charts, markers. Figure out who will run the meeting. You may want to have one of the group (or your coach) run things so you can participate and have time to think about what's being said.

8. Own the results. One thing my group told me was that they were there to help me create *my agenda*. I needed to be comfortable with, as well as committed to, any strategies or goals that might come out of the discussion.

FROM THE TRENCHES

When Brilliance Fails

Sometimes when we actively invite others to critique us, to our chagrin we realize that even when we think we are dead right, we can be dead wrong. Here's the story of a brilliant man who learned this the hard way.

K. served as the executive director of a venerable advocacy organization. I had approached him about running for elected office because I believed he would bring a needed perspective as well as deep knowledge on important issues. He and I had worked together years before, and I knew his strengths—which is why I approached him about running—but I also knew his weaknesses. With a privileged upbringing and a degree from a prestigious university, K. fell into a common trap: he figured that because he was smart and successful, his ideas were always right. He often dismissed others and their ideas, sometimes ruthlessly. I talked frankly to him about this before he ran. I shared what I'd learned, why it was important to listen, how my work was enriched and strengthened by what I had learned from others. I cautioned him that, although he was smart, he could always learn from others' perspectives and ideas.

He won his election. After he was sworn in, I asked him to join a task force I led, knowing his interest in the issue. I had recruited advocates and experts from agencies and businesses to serve on the task force. K. cared deeply about this issue and was excited to jump in and share his ideas. However, convinced as he was that his ideas were the best (and therefore the only) approach, his first act was to try to get the task force to stop considering all the other strategies they had already developed. Other members of the task force told him that they were fine with adding his idea to the list but would continue working on a range of options. He insisted they drop all others in favor of his. As the chair of the task force, I finally had to pull rank. I gave him a choice: support all the work of the task force, not just his own idea, or get off. Faced with this choice, he stopped insisting on his idea as the only way forward. We ended up with a lot of innovative ideas to test out, including K.'s idea, which we moved forward and integrated into the agency's work. Over the next five years, he kept promoting his original proposal on his own, to the exclusion of the other recommendations. He struggled to get support from the rest of the council or from other advocates. It was hard for me to watch a brilliant man be so ineffective. So certain of the rightness of his ideas, he seemed unable to accept that others' ideas could also be good approaches to solving the problem. He left office halfway through his second term, with little to show for his six years on the council.

OPEN HEART, OPEN MIND

In my life as an activist and an elected official I try to keep K.'s story front and center in my thoughts. It is very easy to see both problems and solutions from only one vantage point, your own. It's a very basic human truth: people really do see the world differently. Our perspective derives from our genetics, our life experiences and the thinking of our friends and families. Forgetting this and thinking that other people see the world just as you do is a quick route to frustration. This really became clear to me when I went from advocating to being an elected official. As an advocate, I was free to pursue my own agenda. I was surrounded by people who focused on the same set of goals because I had recruited them or they had been attracted by a vision reflecting my perspective. In office, I suddenly had to work on things other than what motivated me to run. Like collecting garbage and running a zoo. I had to work with a greater variety of people with their own objectives and ideas. Even though everyone was working on the same issues, there were wide variations in how people defined them and what they saw as possible solutions based on their individual perspectives, histories, and ideas.

For example, as a believer in the benefits of "alternative transportation," I advocated for the position that the solution to traffic congestion was to get people out of their cars. After all, all that driving congested the roads, was costly, made people unhealthy, and polluted the air. Others saw cars and highways quite differently: in their minds, cars offer freedom and independence—therefore, traffic jams were caused by too few highways, not too many. Bicycling and walking were not real transportation solutions and diverted scarce resources.

Once I was seated next to a person I didn't know at a business luncheon. He asked me what I did before I was elected. I told him that I had been an activist. He mumbled something under his breath, gave me an angry glower, and got up and left the table! What, I wondered, did this man think an activist was? Something not very nice, I guess. I wish he had stayed so I could have found out his thoughts on exactly what was so horrible about being an activist.

The world looks different to each of us. We build the world in our minds out of our unique genetic inheritance and personal life experiences. This can cause tremendous frustration and make it difficult to communicate with others: "Why can't you just see? It's right there, clear as day!" It's not easy to remember that our reality is just one of many equally valid versions, all reflecting our individual experiences, culture, and genes. There is tremendous power and beauty in this diversity of perspectives—it is the root of great art and innovative ideas. When many people look at a situation and see it in different ways, our understanding can be enriched (if we let it), and our actions can become more compassionate if we take into account the multitude of human experience and desire.

COMMON SENSE ISN'T NECESSARILY COMMON OR SENSIBLE

Want to end discussion quickly? Just throw out this phrase: "It's just common sense." Many times, appeals to common sense are used as some sort of magic formula to place certain ideas, practices, or policies beyond discussion. What is common sense? Common sense is just a code word for status quo. If our world were perfect, with plenty and social justice for all, a healthy natural environment, and no problems like climate change and resource depletion rapidly approaching critical points, then common sense or keeping to the status quo would be a great strategy. When there is something that needs to change, appealing to common sense is a strategy to derail difficult and necessary discussions. There are a lot of ways to play the "common sense" card, with the same effect. I'm sure you've heard "This is how we do this," "That idea is just impractical," "No one believes that," and "We've already tried it and it didn't work." Any of those sound familiar?

There are two things in life we can count on: change and resistance to change. Today is not like yesterday, and tomorrow will be different from today. Even knowing this, many people find the very idea of change scary. Life is difficult enough already, what with having to make a living and care for our families and all the other obligations and responsibilities we have. We rely on our experiences and what we've been taught to get through each day. The desire to avoid change isn't limited to those in power or those who benefit from the status quo. People may oppose change in their communities because they believe that keeping things like they are, even if not perfect, is better than risking change and its unknown consequences. Sometimes people will reject suggestions for changes simply because they are suggested by a person or group outside of their community or from a different culture or perspective. In the short term, rejecting new ideas and different perspectives is just plain easier than figuring out something new.

Here's an example from history. Most community activists dutifully read Saul Alinsky's *Rules for Radicals*, a book that set the standard for community organizing in this country. A key tenet of Alinsky's thought is "let the community lead." The danger in adhering to this is that the activist has no ability to challenge unjust actions supported by the community, even when clearly based on bias and prejudice. This principle of always letting the community lead resulted in some Alinsky-inspired groups opposing the desegregation of neighborhoods in Chicago during the 1960s. Members of those communities felt threatened by efforts to allow African Americans to live in their neighborhoods. Did any of the organizers speak up and challenge the "common sense" idea that separating people based on skin color was a good thing? Did they challenge the community to look beyond its fears and prejudices? I don't know. I do know that we are all enriched by creating a culture where it is okay to challenge each other's ideas, asking ourselves and others to continually examine why we hold the beliefs we have. Are they based on our values and facts? Or are we just repeating patterns of the past? Our communities are stronger when we don't accept common sense as sufficient justification for opposing change or continuing existing policies and actions.

You may be an activist, part of an organization trying to change the world, but you are also a citizen. As a citizen, you have a right to your own concerns and ideas about the world. You are not just a messenger or an empty vessel waiting to be filled by others' concerns and ideas. The beauty of working with others is how ideas ferment and take on new and wonderful forms when we challenge ideologies, prejudices, and preconceptions, including our own. Your work includes sharing your ideas, questioning, listening, and co-creating. Being willing to change who we are—how we see, think, and feel—gives us the power to change the world.

FROM THE TRENCHES

Blinded by Common Sense

In North Portland, previous segregationist policies like redlining and discriminatory real estate practices resulted in some census tracts approaching a fifty percent African American population, making it one of the city's most diverse neighborhoods today. The area is changing rapidly as more and more people return to the city to live. Home prices are rising as crime and gang activity decrease. Many families who lived here for decades moved out—some taking advantage of higher property values and fair housing legislation to move to other neighborhoods. Low-income renters left as rents steadily rose. Many of those moving in were young and many use bicycles for transportation. The community is bisected by a one-way couplet, connecting the neighborhood to the jobs and the fun stuff happening in downtown. Bicycle volumes on these streets were among the highest in the city, and because they were also heavily used by car commuters to bypass congestion on a nearby freeway, conflicts with cars were increasing. Because heavy traffic is noisy, dangerous, and dirty, the livability and desirability of the whole area was severely impacted. The city proposed converting a car traffic lane into a bike lane and encountered the usual opposition, which argued that this proposal proved that the city was anticar. What was unusual was that some members of the African American community also opposed the project. They saw it benefiting the new, predominantly white residents—not existing residents. In their minds, bicycle riding was a "white" phenomenon. Since African Americans didn't ride bikes—or only rode on the sidewalks, as one resident explained—any bicycle improvements necessarily benefited only white people. One African American leader—a former state senator—called the proposed bicycle lanes a "white arrow into the heart of the Black community."

"Common sense" said that African Americans don't ride bicycles. Common sense said that bicycles were toys and not transportation. Common sense said that the status quo—with its heavy, high-speed traffic—was better than an unknown future. Even cycling advocates had their own "common sense" blinders on, insisting that there couldn't be anything racist about transportation decisions, especially such ecologically friendly proposals as bike lanes, ignoring the community's anger over fifty years of highway projects tearing up the community and filling the neighborhoods with commuter traffic.

To its credit, the city took a major step back from implementing the project, although this angered many cycling advocates. The city convened a series of community meetings with the goal of broadening the discussion. Instead of focusing narrowly on design details of the proposed project—the subject of previous meetings that had ended in angry shouting and accusations of forced gentrification and racism—these meetings began with asking the community to participate in defining the problem. They found that they could agree that there were too many cars traveling too fast through their neighborhood. The neighbors shared a common goal: to make their community a safer, quieter, and better place to live. *People who had been divided over the what and how came together over the why and what for.* Everyone could agree on the need to slow down and reduce traffic. They could even agree that something should be done to make cycling safer for the thousands of cyclists using these streets every day. Stepping away from debating a solution helped people focus on the problem. This allowed them to reach the next step: designing solutions that addressed everyone's concerns.

Opening our hearts and minds to other perspectives isn't easy. We are trained to defend our ideas and positions. Our ideas may seem self-evident because our peers and coworkers share them. Or we may have read about them on our favorite websites or in our favorite magazines. But think about it. Everyone else in the room probably thinks the same way about their ideas. That no matter what the subject, they already know what the problem is and how to fix it. Like you, they think their ideas are just common sense. You see what a mess we can get ourselves into!

Opening up conversations that get people to give up their preconceived notions can be tough to do, *but only because we have so little practice examining our own prejudices and biases.* Creating authentic dialogue is one of the most important roles of any leader. And as a leader you need to be self-aware enough to know that you will have the same tendency to sacrifice open dialogue because you want to be efficient. You may assume there is a consensus and want to get going. Most of us start off thinking that we already know what the problem is and what to do about it, thus your work as a leader is to get people to step back and examine the situation with open and inquiring minds. Indeed, this is the greatest contribution a leader can make: challenging common sense by giving everyone a role in defining the problem as well as creating solutions. The next time you are meeting about a contentious idea, in which preconceived opinions are flying, try the following steps:

1. Don't lead with solutions yourself or let others do so. Ask everyone to set his or her solutions aside for a while. If people get too anxious, ask them to take three minutes and write down their concerns. Another good exercise is to ask people at the very beginning to write down the three things they most value in their lives. This helps them step back from the immediate issue and resets their thinking in a positive way.

2. The first question you should ask is "What do you think the problem is here?" Write all the answers on a flip chart or blackboard. Let everyone see the range of perspectives. Just this will get people thinking in new ways.

3. Ask people to explain their thinking around the problem as they see it. Who is affected? Are some groups benefiting from the current situation? Is there a way to gauge the level of threat? Are there connections between problems the group has identified? Group similar ideas together.

4. Have the group brainstorm solutions to each problem, focusing especially on those deemed a higher threat and with a high level of connectedness. If you have a large group, break into groups no bigger than ten and set ground rules so that everyone has a chance to listen and to speak.

5. Ask whether there are solutions that the group can see endorsing. If not, what changes might they suggest to make the solutions more acceptable?

BUT BEWARE OF UNCOMMON SENSE, TOO!

When you are new to the game, you can get a lot a pressure to defer to the experts. After all, the experts do have a lot of training and experience, so it can seem only natural to think that they really do know better. What experts bring to the table is often "uncommon" sense, if you will, in that most people won't have the deep knowledge of a specific field they have. Of course, that's why we hire experts in the first place. But the more specialized their education and knowledge are, the narrower their perspective on the world tends to be and the more difficulty they have accepting other perspectives. The world is much richer and more complex than any one discipline can hope to encompass. If we limit ourselves to solutions prescribed by experts in one narrow discipline, we miss opportunities to be innovative, inclusive, and responsive. Remember, experts are human, too, with biases and personal values that affect how they see the world, despite their training and experience in their particular field. Hidden by jargon and authoritative pronouncements, an expert's individual value judgments and the influence they have on their analysis and recommendations are rarely recognized.

They can greatly affect how experts define problems, as well as what they offer as solutions. Expecting experts to provide clear and understandable explanations of their underlying assumptions is the first step in demystifying what they do—and a good way to begin empowering citizens. The next step is to have the community create the values and outcomes that the experts will use to analyze conditions and measure the effectiveness of their recommended solutions.

- The City of Portland had been dumping raw sewage into the Willamette River every time it rained—and it rains a lot in Portland. This was because when the sewers were first built, in the late 1800s, storm water and sewage were run into the same system. As Portland grew and more land was paved over, every time it rained there was just too much water for the sewage treatment plant to handle. Sued by a local environmental group to comply with the federal Clean Water Act prohibiting discharging raw sewage into the river, the city came up with an ambitious plan to solve the problem by building giant underground tunnels to store this water and then release it slowly to the sewage treatment center. After spending $1.4 billion and taking ten years, the project was finished. But it wasn't enough! Continued growth and development meant more rainwater went into the sewer. High sewer bills caused by the project led to a ratepayer revolt, including a citizen initiative to strip the bureau from city oversight. The city rethought the problem and came up with a new solution. Pushed by green advocates, they came up with a plan to plant eighty thousand trees, pay people to disconnect downspouts from the sewer and build green roofs, and build bio-swales along streets to divert rainwater into the soil rather than into the sewer. Total cost: just a bit more than $1 million in public funds a year for five years.
- Traffic engineers rate traffic using an A–F scale they call Level of Service. The F grade is easy to understand: full gridlock. Stuck in traffic. A road with little or no traffic gets an A grade. Most city streets are typically rated D or E. Always wanting to get a good grade, for over fifty years, federal,

state, and local governments have spent trillions of dollars to try to make all our roads "A" roads. Somewhere back in time, an anonymous traffic engineer decided that the highest value for a road is moving traffic really fast. So a crowded road gets a failing grade. An empty road gets an A. This person's value of vehicle speed and mobility over all else is built into traffic models all over the country and is rarely questioned. It ignores the fact that higher speeds result in more and worse crashes. Or that high-speed roads divide communities, lower property values, and encourage more driving. In fact, empty roads are just a big waste of money. The experts have made our cities expensive, dangerous, sprawling, and socially destructive. And all despite being told decades ago by brilliant thinkers like Jane Jacobs, in her book *The Life and Death of Great American Cities*, that, for cities to prosper and be good places to live, streets need to be welcoming to *people*.

- Mandates for school reform have burdened local school districts with a multitude of expensive and ever-changing demands, including funding tied to testing. Many programs such as art, music, and physical education have been cut. Recess has been eliminated. All to give kids more seat time. Yet test scores and high school graduation rates remain dismal after more than thirty years of these reform efforts. Multiple studies demonstrate conclusively that when children are physically active, even just running around and jumping, their brains develop much better. Getting outside during the day increases brain functioning and reduces behavioral problems. Human bodies and human brains are a whole, and children's mental as well as physical development is stunted if they are not allowed to play. And playing out of doors is better still. Yet the experts insist that more hours of seat time will result in more academic success, despite a mountain of evidence to the contrary.

Do these stories mean we should fire all the experts? Heck, no! Engineers and other experts are invaluable for helping design solutions—laying out the how. What they aren't as good at is deciding the why and the what. Those are decisions that rightfully belong to us citizens. It may seem easier to "just let the experts decide." It can seem so rational when the answer is presented with all the bells and whistles of jargon and data carried to the fourth decimal place. But it's a big mistake. Don't leave the future to experts! Don't avoid the difficult, yet critical, discussions about who benefits and who pays. Don't let the experts and their set of values (no matter how well disguised) decide what is best for your community. Leaders bring the community's aspirations and values to the surface. When this is done, after the public deliberates and debates and decides what is important, then it's time to ask the experts to help design solutions that respect and further our values. They can do it. They are good at this part of the process. We just have to give them direction and hold them accountable to ensure that it is the community's values that drive the process.

BEING COMFORTABLE WITH UNCERTAINTY

One thing that sticks with me after many years of community activism and twelve years in elected office is that *there never really is a single answer to many of the questions and problems we face.* Because the world is constantly changing, our understanding of challenges and how to respond to those challenges has to change, too. We learn new stuff. New people want to be at the table. A solution that once worked may be ineffective under new conditions or even harm us. Building bigger highways to solve traffic jams only caused more driving. Eliminating recess only made our kids bored and fat. Burning coal and oil threatens to destroy human civilization. Yet constantly reexamining our actions can be difficult and unsettling. Most people prefer to make a decision and stick with it, especially if the process of coming to an answer was difficult. Ensuring the new information and perspectives are considered is the role of a leader.

Conservatism—belief in the value of traditional and established practices in society and politics—was a great evolutionary strategy when our ancestors lived in a world that didn't change much for hundreds or even thousands of years. Today we daily witness how humans are changing the face of the earth. Seven billion people want to live good lives, but the strategies that served us for centuries when many fewer of us were on the planet—clear-cutting forests; dumping waste from factory, farm, and city into the water and air; fishing until all the fish are gone—don't only produce diminishing returns, they threaten to kill us. Our habitual conservatism is leading us into danger. Our task in this century is to question and change our habits, including policies, behaviors, and technologies, to ensure that the ways we live are actually making our lives better and not making our problems worse.

Not being able to rely on the tried-and-true is a great challenge to our society. It is also a challenge to each of us personally. But it can also be liberating to realize we have permission, indeed a responsibility, to seek out innovative solutions to problems. And people love to be asked to be creative! We don't have to know everything, to be the smartest in the room, or to hold tightly on to our opinions. Because the world is changing so fundamentally and common sense is so obviously failing us, we are free to seek solutions that fit the moment we live in, enriched by the multiple realities of diverse communities. In fact, our lives depend on it.

LEARNING TO LISTEN

Part of being a politician or activist is being a social butterfly, flitting from meeting to awards dinner to community meeting to coffee shop. Especially for a politician, a big part of the work is showing up at all sorts of occasions out in the community. These are great chances to meet new people. I really enjoy them. I get to try out new foods, meet interesting people, and most importantly hear new perspectives. One of the biggest Aha! moments in my career was when I realized that achieving my goals depended on actively engaging with others.[1]

---

1. My advice to current or potential elected officials: don't parachute in and out of community events—you'll be the one missing out. A community event is a chance to open *your* mind. Sit down, have a plate of beans and rice, chat with the person next to you, listen to the choir, hear the presentation, participate in the workshop. Be there as a participant. Don't check your email. (No matter how discreet you are, people can tell when you aren't paying attention.) Be present for as long as you are there.

This can get tiring, always being in demand. But community events are often more useful and rewarding than many official meetings! The creativity out there is amazing. Don't rush discovery: you are the ears and antennae of your organization, harvesting ideas and relationships in ways that more formal outreach can't. Way too often well-meaning people, in headlong pursuit of very worthy goals, get tripped up. Because they are so eager to implement a solution, they spend their time pushing their ideas rather than listening to the community, discovering new ideas, and even making new friends. Friends, connections, and ideas make the difference between success and failure.

Why listen? Because you never know when you'll hear an idea that changes your perspective in a way that leads to a better solution. Many times the most unlikely people will give you amazing and perspective-changing ideas, if you are open to hearing them. A variety of ideas thrown into the hopper can help develop richer strategies. Not every encounter results in a revelation, of course. But when it happens, the impact can be considerable. Even if you don't have an Aha! moment, when you take the time to really listen to others you get a new appreciation for the richness and wonder of the human experience.

By engaging with others, you will get firsthand insight into how the abstract impacts people's lives. Statistics often obscure people's real lives and stories. The more educated we are and the more accustomed we are to using data to make our arguments, the harder it is to understand this. Politics (and I include activism in my definition of politics) is about *people* and how our decisions affect their lives. It is our job to constantly think about how the decisions we make can make everyone's life better. Hearing people's stories—their yearnings and even their prejudices—injects humanity and compassion into the civic process. When we listen, really listen, we will become stronger leaders. By reflecting our whole community—with its many wonderful and various strands—we become better people.

TRY IT NOW #5

Hearing Other Voices, Writing Their Stories

There are two strategies that I've found effective in getting others to authentically engage. Depending on whether you are a people person or more of a shy type, pick one of the strategies below and use it the next time you are working with a group of people. Write down what you learn. Consider starting a "story log." This can be as simple as keeping a small spiral notebook handy to jot notes in or even writing yourself a memo on your smartphone. Knowing you will be writing down what you recall will help you listen more intently. As you keep writing your story log, you can track whether your skill in capturing the essence of what you hear improves. These stories will come in handy as inspiration and even as promotional copy as you put together articles, business cases, grant applications, and so on (with your subjects' permission, of course!).

1. For the extroverts and type A personalities reading this book (you know who you are!): Ask people directly to tell you their stories. You can be very specific, probing the issue or problem at hand and asking them to describe how it personally affects them or their family or community. Ask them to make it personal rather than abstract, focusing on what the problem is rather than arguing for their solution. When your intent is to win someone's trust, ask them about their family, how they grew up, or what their children are like (their ages, their interests, their neighborhood). Then share your own story—you will both be amazed at the parallels in your stories!

2. If you are a shy person, you may not be comfortable asking people directly. You can still become better at engaging others and drawing out their stories. Try this: Ask a group of people—a committee you are part of, the PTA board, a group you volunteer with—to share stories with each other, in groups of two. For example, when we brought people together at the launching of the Coalition for a Livable Future, most of the people in the room had never worked with each other. So, at

the start of every meeting, we would pair off—with someone we didn't know—and ask our partners to answer a question, different each time. For example, at one meeting where the topic was affordable housing, we asked everyone to tell their partners a story about how housing affordability had affected their lives. They had two minutes to share their stories, then the other person got to speak while they listened. People shared very personal stories, some heartbreaking, some hilarious, all giving some insight into how their lives were affected by housing costs. Because we had committed to building understanding and connection in this intimate and very human way, in subsequent debates over goals and strategies, the whole group behaved differently: more respectfully, more thoughtfully.

I love a good book. I can get lost in stories that range from crazy science fiction and fantasy to ancient history. A good writer can convey the human drama of meeting challenges and living to others. Maybe you love movies. Or you like to sit around a campfire and shoot the breeze. What links gossip to high literature is our natural interest in other people. How they live their lives. Who they love. How they overcome obstacles. Leaders can utilize our affection for storytelling to help people see what they share—hopes, fears, values—and create new stories to bring communities together to envision and achieve a better world for us all to live in.

CHAPTER 2 BLUEPRINT FOR CHANGE

In this chapter I've discussed the personal challenges of leadership, including managing your time and your emotions as well as opening up your ears and mind. In exploring these personal challenges I showed you how to:

- Gain perspective and center yourself using lessons from two thousand years ago to be a more effective activist today.
- "Think the Worst First" to clear your mind so you can do your best.
- Prepare for opportunity and serendipity by knowing yourself.

- Find help from colleagues and coaches.

- Create a community brain trust to help you set goals and cope with challenges.

- Be counterintuitive and discover the ways that brilliance, common sense, and expertise can foil your plans.

- Use stories and listening to keep an open heart and open mind and cultivate the ability to power through in spite of constant uncertainty.

CHAPTER 3

ASKING FOR HELP: GETTING OTHERS ON BOARD

"We're better together than we are apart. The American Dream has us looking out for ourselves even at the expense of our neighbors. That shit ain't true, man."
—*Trevor D. Richardson, founder of the* Subtopian *magazine*

If you really want to make a difference, if you really want to make things happen, you are going to need help. By bringing others into your project, you will learn new skills, be introduced to exciting new perspectives, and probably enjoy the work more, in addition to receiving help to achieve your goals.

My great-grandparents left Sweden in the late 1800s and settled in Kansas. They were farmers, and they and many of their neighbors left Sweden after suffering a number of years of failed crops and hunger during what was known in northern Europe as "the years without summer." They didn't know that on the other side of the world a mountain had blown up (Krakatoa in Indonesia), filling the atmosphere with ash and cooling the planet. All these farmers knew was that they needed to leave their home, hoping for a better life in the United States. Along with traditional dishes like lutefisk, they brought strong traditions of working together. Together, these new Americans built a church that still stands. Together, they built and funded a public school, one of the first in Kansas. Together, they founded a college to train teachers, where, until the 1930s, Swedish was the language of instruction. They pooled their resources and shared their labor. Before big machines did our work for us, our forebears tackled big projects, like putting up barns or harvesting their crops, with the whole community pitching in. They simply had to. Everyone's wheat ripened at about the same time and had to be harvested quickly. By coming together to do a big job, they had the advantage of combining many people's skills, perspectives, and experiences as well as their labor. I remember my grandparents saying, "Many hands make light work," the real meaning of which I didn't understand until I learned this history later in life. I thought it was just a way to get us kids to pitch in on chores!

Many of our familiar institutions began as communal projects. In addition to schools and churches, the insurance industry got its start when members of a particular community paid into a common fund to cover those infrequent but expensive inevitabilities of life, such as fires, funerals, and caring for widows and orphans. The Odd Fellows. The Elks. The Woodsmen of the World. The traditional cooperative approach is still practiced in many immigrant communities today as members of these groups combine their resources to help each other succeed in a new country and culture.

Today, few of us would think of building our own homes, much less starting a college. Farming is done mostly by large corporations with giant, expensive equipment. Work is increasingly about being connected to a computer rather than to other people. *We are out of practice asking for help or expecting to be asked.* This makes it difficult for us to realize that we can call on others when we need help or want to fix problems beyond our capabilities. When we look, we will find many others who are also looking at the world and its problems and want to help.

"If you never ask, how can anyone ever say yes?"

Those are some of the most powerful words I have ever heard. I repeat them often (especially when people shudder at the thought of fund-raising). That question reminds us that people really want to help. Most will respond enthusiastically *but only if they are asked*. People are incredibly generous in America:[2]

- 95.4% of households give to charity.
- The average annual household contribution is $2,974.
- Americans gave $335.17 billion in 2013 (this reflects a 4.4% increase from 2011).
- In 2013, the largest source of charitable giving came from individuals, at $241.32 billion, or 72% of total giving.
- 64.5 million adults volunteered a total of 7.9 billion hours of service, worth an estimated value of $175 billion.
- In 2013, there were approximately 1,500,000 charitable organizations in the United States.

When you ask for help you will rapidly discover that you aren't alone. Many others are concerned about many of the same problems you are and will respond willingly to requests for help, advice, and even money. When you ask, you'll find yourself surrounded by people who will do more for you than just share the load. Working with others will sharpen your thinking, broaden your perspective, and help you communicate more effectively. Working with others will give a big boost to your efforts as well as your sense of satisfaction because many hands really do make light work.

---

2.   Source: National Philanthropic Trust, www.nptrust.org

READY, SET, STOP

You need help. There is always much more to do than you can do yourself. Recognizing that is the first step toward success. But before you rush out like Superman or Wonder Woman to rally the forces of good and save the day, do a little looking around your community. Are there others doing similar work you can ally with? Surveying who is out there can save the time and effort that it takes to start a new movement. It can also lead to productive and innovative alliances. Don't be so narrow in your vision that you miss potential allies or waste time creating a whole new effort or organization that duplicates what someone else is already doing. Here are some of the ways you can find allies and partners, often by just tapping on your laptop or picking up your phone:

- Look online to find others connected with the issue and talk with them.
- See if national groups working on these issues have a local chapter.
- Look for groups that might be natural partners with your cause—this may include schools, museums, and other nonprofits.
- Find out which elected officials or agency staff deal with your issue and call them up; they can direct you to others interested in the same thing.
- A good way to find out who is doing what in your community is researching who local foundations are funding. The Foundation Center has a free searchable database full of good info.
- Look into a national network of progressive foundations called the Funding Exchange (fex.org). They may have an affiliated foundation in your state with a list of potential contacts.
- Read your local newspaper and look for information on local events and fundraisers as well as news on your particular topic.

Finally, never discount the importance of good old-fashioned word-of-mouth networking. Mention your interest to acquaintances, friends, colleagues, and family members. ("Hi, How are you? What are you up to?" "Well, I'm really concerned about X and wondering how to get involved in helping address it. Do you have any advice?") Ask if they know of existing groups or if they would be interested in helping you build a new movement or pitching in on a one-time event. Remember your elevator speech (from TRY IT NOW #1) and use it.

FROM THE TRENCHES

Same Goal, Different Actions

Almost from the first arrival of Europeans on this continent, some of the newcomers, inspired and awed by this place's natural beauty, argued for preserving some of it from development. Writers and activists from Thoreau to John Muir to Rachel Carson challenged those who saw America simply as trees to cut, ore to mine, land to plow. Today, there are many organizations working to save and restore natural areas. Two of these groups are the Nature Conservancy and the Sierra Club. They have similar goals, but their tactics are quite different, and the debate over which of their approaches is the best sometimes gets hot.

The Sierra Club: Founded in California in 1892 by John Muir, the Sierra Club led efforts to protect some of the natural wonders of America by establishing and expanding America's system of national parks, including Yosemite, Glacier, and Mount Rainier National Parks. The Club's hard but losing fight to prevent damming the Hetch Hetchy Valley in the Sierra Nevadas (likened to Yosemite for its dramatic landscape) to provide drinking water for San Francisco was the first split between preservationists and conservationists. Conservationists supported the continued use of natural resources, albeit with a gentler touch, while preservationists thought that enough of the world had been logged and mined, and stopping further development of wild areas was the only responsible position. The Club intensified its preservationist and adversarial approach under David Brower in the 1960s. Spurred by plans to dam the Colorado River and flood the Grand Canyon, Brower persuaded the board of the Sierra Club to use strategies ranging from lawsuits, massive public relations campaigns, protests, and eventually civil disobedience to oppose many threats to the environment. Brower's position was based on the idea that environmental victories are temporary, while environmental losses are permanent. Under his leadership, the Sierra Club adopted a very activist, some would say aggressive, style of advocacy to preserve nature.

The Nature Conservancy: Taking a different approach to protecting natural areas, the Nature Conservancy works with private landowners, companies, and governments to acquire land and conservation easements to protect critical habitat or natural values from development or resource extraction. Founded in 1951 and led by a former Wall Street executive, its market-based approach relies on negotiation, major fund-raising efforts, and savvy real estate skills. It has chapters in all fifty states as well as in many countries. Their record is impressive; as of 2014, the Nature Conservancy has "protected more than 119 million acres of land and 5,000 river miles" and it operates "more than 100 marine conservation projects globally." In comparison, US national parks comprise eighty-four million acres, and federal wilderness areas add another 110 million areas of protected lands.

So, which approach is more effective? Both groups' missions address climate change, sustainable energy, and nature-friendly development. The Sierra Club generally appeals to more proregulatory activists, while the Nature Conservancy can count many market-oriented supporters. You will meet people whose ideas as well as favored approaches are similar to yours. You will also encounter many who share your goals but believe that different strategies are more effective. There are many ways to cook an egg.

SURVIVING YOUR FIRST MEETING

When I went pro as an activist—actually getting paid to advocate—I was almost giddy to discover that just about every government agency and bureau had a meeting they wanted me—me!—to come to. The calls came in so frequently that we had a joke among ourselves that we should set up a hotline called Meetings Anonymous; if you found yourself with a night free, you could call in and find some meeting, any meeting, to go to! While being willing to serve on an advisory committee or attend a hearing on an issue you care about is part and parcel of being a good citizen and activist, to really drive your agenda you need to take charge.

And that usually means calling a meeting of your own.

In your own meeting, you set the agenda. You get to decide what you hope to achieve, who to invite, who gets to talk, and what message you want to be heard. Even the where and the when of a meeting can be significant.

That said, putting on your first meeting can be a scary thing. How do you decide what to talk about as well as who should do the talking? Where do you advertise, and what are ways to get people interested enough to give up their precious free time? What if no one shows up? Here is some practical guidance on making your meetings successful:

Step 1. Answer the question, why are you calling a meeting? A meeting is a good way to recruit volunteers, whether to plant trees or to canvass the neighborhood for a candidate or to do any other big project. A public meeting is a good way to raise awareness about your issue and create broad community support for action. Or you want to hold community leaders accountable by hosting a public forum on a particular issue. Knowing why you are asking people to show up will shape how you set up and run your meeting.

Step 2. Decide who you want to show up, and design the meeting for your target group. Are you looking for people with specific skills or connections, or do you just need lots of bodies? Is it a negotiation or a rally? You'll want to pick a setting that fits the purpose. A strategy session or an event to recruit board members will be an intimate get-together; a coffee shop or a restaurant will work well. Fighting city hall and want a crowd? Schools, community centers, and libraries are some of the places that have meeting rooms available for free or at low cost. You can get a room at a college or government agency if someone who works there sponsors the meeting.

Step 3. Prepare for your meeting. Too many people call a meeting and expect it to just happen. Maybe you've attended one of these—they tend to start late, there isn't a clear agenda, and you have trouble finding the location. This doesn't get you too excited to help out.

- Pick a convenient time. After all, you want people to show up, and if the people you want there have to work, go to church, or deal with childcare at the time you've chosen, they won't be there.

- Make sure there is good transit access or the meeting place is otherwise easy to get to.

- Lay out a clear agenda, detailing the purpose of the meeting, what you hope to accomplish during the meeting, and start and stop times. Designate roles such as facilitator, timekeeper, and scribe, and include contact information. Include ground rules to govern discussion.

- Get the word out. I first met the people who would start the Bicycle Transportation Alliance when I read a flyer posted on a telephone pole. There are many more ways to do this today, including creating Facebook events, sending text messages, placing notices in community newspapers (beware of the long lead time they require), putting up posters at public places like cafés and libraries, and using resources like Meetup and Craigslist. Then there is the tried and trusted technique: asking people in person or by phone. If you want a particular person or group to show up, call them. People love to be invited, and nothing says they matter like a personal phone call or message. If this seems like too much work, create a phone tree at your first meeting and have everyone call five of their friends for the next one.

Step 4. Run your meeting with confidence. Whether two or fifty people show up, they are there because they care about the same thing you do, so relax!

- Say hello. Take the time for introductions. If it's a small group, ask people to say their name, why they came, and something else about themselves. No speeches here! Ask everyone to take just a minute. I recently started a group out by asking them an additional question: If you could take a selfie with anyone, famous or not, living or not, who might it be? Introductions in a larger group, say, over fifteen, could eat up all your time, so try one of these: Ask them to turn to someone in the group they don't know and introduce themselves with the same set of questions. You can even add in the selfie exercise. Five minutes is plenty of time for this. In really big groups, make requests related to your topic, for example, "Raise your hand if you've ever been stopped by the police" or "Raise your hand if your favorite tree is a Norway maple. Or how about a ginkgo?"

- Introduce yourself and other members of your planning team.

- Thank everyone for coming.

- Go over the agenda, emphasizing your purpose in asking people to come. Be clear that the agenda is there to help guide the meeting and can change to meet the group's needs.

- Go over the ground rules for an effective meeting. If you have time, ask the group to suggest their own ways they prefer to interact with others. There are many variations of this easily found on the Web, but they all include these:

  - Respect others' opinions.

  - One person speaks at a time.

  - Encourage everyone to participate.

  - Focus questions on clarifying rather than challenging.

- Recap at the end, including any conclusions the group may have come to, commitments made, next steps, and how to stay involved. Thank everyone for coming again.

- Start and end on time.

Step 5. Follow up. Follow up, follow up, follow up. Do what you said you would do and help others to follow through on their commitments, as well. This means getting everyone's name, contact numbers, and email. Before everyone leaves the room, enlist the most fervent volunteer to coordinate volunteers for you.

FINDING THE LEADERS IN THE ROOM

Here's a secret: leaders may be sitting anywhere in the room. Someone sitting quietly in the back of the room may not appear to be very engaged, but this may be their style of participating, not a sign they are not interested. Some people sit in the back because they are shy. Or they are comfortable letting others lead the discussions, saving their contribution until after they have had some time to reflect. I've seen meetings take completely new directions or come to unexpected resolution after the person who had been sitting quietly spoke her piece.

Conversely, many people attend meetings, whether at work or in their community, and never speak up. They may be afraid to speak up because they don't feel welcome, they don't know the rules (spoken and unspoken), or they worry that their ideas will appear stupid or silly. Others, skeptical of the process or the conveners, may wonder whether their contributions will really be heard. I wonder how much good thinking is missed out on because too many of us compete aggressively for airtime or try to "score points" for the cleverest rhetoric or best-phrased put-downs of others' ideas.

A well-run meeting can go a long way toward helping shy or intimidated people make meaningful contributions. Setting and enforcing clear ground rules helps overcome both shyness and skepticism. The challenge I want to pose to you now is how to discover those who have leadership abilities but are not engaging with the process. The truth is that we all need all the help we can get. By encouraging effective, thoughtful people to engage, your work will be easier and more successful.

The next time you are in a meeting of any sort, whether a casual gathering in a coffee shop, a public hearing, or a meeting you've convened, make it a point to observe the others in the room, paying particular attention to facial expressions and body language. Note where people choose to sit. Are they up front, sitting upright on the edge of their chair, or hanging out in the back of the room? When people speak, are their comments thoughtful, respectful of others, building on the ideas of others? Do others pay attention, nod their heads, or otherwise affirm what they are hearing? Who volunteers to help? Do they follow through? Find out why this person came and what they hope to see happen.

You know what you are looking for, right? Someone who is thoughtful, respected, willing to contribute, and interested in your issue. Someone who, with a little encouragement and an invitation, will join in and help. That help can come in many forms: connecting you with new communities by vouching for your good intentions, introducing you to other influential people such as potential funders or political support, offering to partner with you to move your shared agenda forward.

Remember that this process is a two-way street, and others will also be assessing you and critiquing you for your integrity, commitment, and inclusivity. Being open to people and their ideas is a quality you are looking for in others—they are looking for the same in you.

DON'T PUT THE FURNITURE IN CHARGE

If you wish to deepen your allies' commitment, empower them. Don't just ask them what they would like to see happen but engage them in deciding *how decisions will be made* about what to do to achieve their vision. Often, how we discuss issues and make decisions has a big impact on what information, values, and choices end up being taken seriously. Asking the community for help in creating decision-making and goal-setting processes creates opportunities for new ideas and perspectives to be heard and serves to balance out the power of those who are used to speaking up and talking "loud."

Let me give you an example. My son walked into his fourth-grade classroom and faced an unsettling and challenging sight: his teacher had taken all the chairs and tables and piled them in a big pile right in the middle of the room. The walls were blank. There were no inspirational posters, no calendars framed with scalloped bric-a-brac, no lists of vocabulary words to memorize. Nothing he expected to see on the first day of school. His teacher stood there in shorts—a teacher in shorts!—welcoming him and his classmates into the room. What was going on? Where were the neat rows of desks? Where was he supposed to sit?

His teacher, John, waited until the classroom was filled with students and then asked them, "How do you want to learn this year?" His job, he told them, was to help them learn, not to teach them. And the learning process began with having them decide, as a group, how the classroom should be set up. How to arrange the chairs and desks, or even whether to use chairs and desks at all! He told them that he wasn't going to sit at a desk himself—his computer was on a shelf in the corner. The kids started learning in that moment. They had to problem-solve together. They learned to speak as well as listen. They had to figure out who among their classmates was thoughtful, who was dictatorial, and who chose to be uninvolved. Because John said they would only move ahead when the class came to an agreement, they had to figure out ways to negotiate and compromise if they were ever going to be able to sit down!

Think of my son's story the next time you meet, whether with one person or one hundred. How might the "furniture" be affecting the quality and tone of your inter-actions? This might literally be about how the furniture is arranged, or it may be how the meeting is run (take a look back at the section "Surviving Your First Meeting"). Have you ever rearranged a meeting room to bring people closer together, say, in an intimate circle rather than a formal lecture-type arrangement? How did people react? Some will be excited and become more animated, while others might grumble uncomfortably, cross their arms over their chests, or even insist on sitting at the back of the room rather than in the circle. Their actions speak volumes about their level of commitment and engagement. We often let furniture arrangement decide how we are going to interact, unconsciously using the room's setup to establish power relationships. Think of how sitting across a big desk or table from someone creates emotional as well as physical distance. Setting chairs in a circle rather than around a table immediately lowers barriers between people, making them more open to others and their ideas.

My son's teacher began his year letting go of his power as a teacher to set the rules and therefore empowering his students, giving them the permission to determine the best way for them to succeed at learning through a process designed to embody learning itself.

VALIDATE THE HUMANITY OF THE "OTHER"

Opening myself to different voices and points of view made me a better and more successful leader. This meant accepting that my own perspectives were narrow and prejudiced—not an easy thing to learn about yourself! As part of my work at Metro, I often attended community events and met with representatives from the many different ethnic communities in Portland. These were great opportunities to learn culturally appropriate ways of connecting with others, reducing my awkwardness when in new situations and making me more effective in communicating and working with people from backgrounds quite different from mine. For example, I learned that many African immigrants prefer to start any conversation by asking about the health and status of family members before talking business. In the Latino community, I learned having a bite to eat, even if just a little, was customary before getting down to the matter at hand. And with African Americans, my success came only after meeting someone whom others in that community trusted and developing a relationship with that person first. He or she could then let others know that, yes, Rex is a good man and is someone we can work with.

My personal style, inherited from my culture, is to focus on getting results with a minimum of time and fuss—being "businesslike." Taking into account and respecting cultural differences wasn't easy for me at first. But now I make a point of asking people about their lives, their families, or hobbies we've discussed before. Even with people I have struggled with, I find that by paying attention to their broader humanity, I can share a laugh or a sad story about life. Recognizing what we share as humans creates common ground upon which to build solutions that meet all our needs.

You might think, "I don't have time to make small talk! So much is wrong with our world that has to be changed RIGHT NOW." But change takes time, often a very long time. You will spend a lot of time working with other people, some of whom you might think of as your opponents, maybe even your "enemies." The people you struggle with might be neighbors living in the same community as you. They have family they care about. Their hopes and aspirations probably aren't all that different from yours. You will see them over and over again. Treating them with respect as fellow humans, even if you're disappointed or angry over a particular decision, will help you be a better advocate as well as a happier person.

TRUSTING LOCAL KNOWLEDGE

As a kid, I liked watching adventure movies, the ones where the explorer sets out to learn about a new country or to discover a city of gold or a lost civilization. If that explorer was smart, he hired a local guide who, despite the lack of education and a complete set of clothes, would predictably (and repeatedly) save the explorer's life from encounters with snakes, dragons, or hostile tribes, or from falling off a cliff. Smug in his superiority, the explorer would do something obviously stupid and then be chagrined when shown how things are done in that country. Or the explorer would charge in and try to bend the country to his will, suffering the consequences of his arrogance and ignorance. While we will survive our ventures into new communities in our work to change the world, we will always be more successful if we seek advice from the community first. Local people know where opportunities as well as difficulties lie.

Keeping the explorer-guide metaphor in mind, take care in choosing your guide. Your goal is to be introduced to a new community, not to exacerbate divisions within it or be "captured" by one particular point of view. Like everyone else, local residents may be unaware of their own preconceptions and prejudices. Just like you, they make assumptions about the world and how it works. They can also jump to conclusions about people's motivations as well as have their own history with other community members. Deepen your understanding of local issues by consulting with a variety of community members. Look at your relationship with your local "guide" as an ongoing chance to learn from each other and to meet others. Listen but also share your perspectives and thoughts. Your outsider perspective and experiences can enrich their understanding of issues, just as their local knowledge will help guide your thinking about problems and solutions.

HOW TO HEAR (NOT FEAR) HATRED

Here's a tough one for you. I know it's really tough for me. All my talk of respect and openness gets tested to the max when having to deal with someone whose ethics or worldview is just so contrary to what I believe that it makes me want to crouch down and cover my ears. In Oregon's last election, there was a ballot measure to remove the ability of people without proper documentation to get a driver's license. Changes in federal law in 2007 made proof of citizenship a requirement for obtaining driver's licenses and other government identification. While some people, such as those without birth certificates, were affected by this, most who sought a legal way to be licensed were undocumented immigrants.

Now, I'm a person who finds variety exciting. I believe immigration is why America is the dynamic country it is today. But do you know what some proponents of this idea said? They carried huge banners in front of one of the main service agencies for immigrants reading: "DIVERSITY IS A CODE WORD FOR WHITE GENOCIDE." Can you believe that? I tell you, I just shut them out. Racism and other expressions of hate are really hard for me to hear. Then I asked myself, "Is it possible to hear others, to understand the fear and anger and find truths that may connect us?"

The key for me is understanding that anger comes from fear. And people get angriest when what they really care about seems threatened. Consider the above example. It has been almost a century since the average person in the US has experienced such economic insecurity. Millions of people lost their homes or carry tremendous debt while fearing for their jobs. Public schools are too often failing our kids, with more than one in four failing to graduate on time. While violent crimes are dropping, the 24-hour media focus on murder and mayhem makes it seem the opposite is happening. I could go on, but you get the point. People are scared for their families, afraid they won't be able to provide for them, and fearful that their children's lives will only get worse. A measure like allowing undocumented people to get driver's licenses raises at least two powerful fears: that the rule of law will be further eroded and that economic opportunities for poor citizens will become even scarcer. And this is exactly what opponents of this measure emphasized.

Although unsuccessful, the Yes campaign on this measure—the side in favor of issuing driver's licenses to people without documentation—took on these fears directly and designed its message around shared values. Their message had three key components: the need of parents to be able to work to provide for their families, the injustice of forcing people to break the law (people would still have to drive, but without a license, they couldn't get auto insurance), and the idea of America as a nation of people who've come here from elsewhere and work hard to make a good life for their families. These are messages about being good members of the community and good family people.

Over fifty years ago, Martin Luther King Jr. gave us this strategic advice for dealing with hatred that is worth remembering today: "Returning hate for hate multiplies hate, adding deeper darkness to a night already devoid of stars. Darkness cannot drive out darkness; only light can do that. Hate cannot drive out hate, only love can do that."

Instead of demonizing those who equated diversity with discrimination and racism against white people, the Yes campaign emphasized what is shared by all Oregonians, and they did it in a way that celebrated these common values and aspirations—messages of love, not hate.

Our history contains many instances of people with different beliefs and interests clashing violently—the Civil War, battles to win living wages in the mines of Appalachia and the Rockies, the struggle to gain civil rights for African Americans. Conflict is intensified during periods of economic turmoil. Uncertainty about what the future holds for us exacerbates many social problems and makes people less accepting of differences and resistant to change. With growing income inequality over the last thirty or forty years, our political discourse is less collaborative and more prone to extremism. Negotiating these differences takes a willingness to set aside our own judgments and prejudices as we seek common ground.

If you've ever been to Oregon or seen pictures of it, you will know that it is very green. With up to 120 inches of precipitation a year, mostly rain, the trees in the western mountains grow huge in what is a temperate rain forest. Think the Amazon without the humidity and piranhas! Huge fortunes were made cutting these trees to build San Francisco (in the gold rush days) and houses throughout the country after World War II. Yet, even with all that rain, trees couldn't grow as fast as they were being cut. As logging companies depleted their timberlands, they pushed to log more and more trees in the national forests. Conservationists pushed back and succeeded in getting some areas set aside as wilderness and passing laws favoring long-term, sustainable harvests over the cut-and-run practices of the big lumber barons. The great recession of the 1980s, along with leveraged buyout-fueled over-logging, crashed Oregon's timber economy. It has taken over thirty years to begin to recover, with far fewer mills and jobs.

The industry still hasn't recovered from its reputation as pillagers of the land, especially as its main harvest technique—clear-cutting—involves cutting every tree over large areas. Hardly a positive image. Certainly not for the majority of Oregonians, who live in cities and only see the forests when they drive through them on vacation, on their way to the beach or mountains.

As you might imagine, people in the timber business are fairly conservative and feel misunderstood by urbanites. They feel unappreciated for their contribution to the state's economy and besieged by new rules and regulations imposed upon them by outsiders. The timber industry set up the Oregon Forest Resources Institute (OFRI) to educate Oregonians on forestry issues. OFRI is funded by a harvest tax on timber. The majority of its board represents major timber companies, including Georgia Pacific, owned by the Koch brothers. Some of these companies fund strident and even vicious political attacks on those they consider too liberal, especially environmental groups.

Now, here is where my story intersects with theirs and where I had to really stretch out of my comfort zone to hear people who I strongly disagree with and who would usually disagree with me.

FROM THE TRENCHES

Even Sworn Enemies Can Find Common Ground

Oregon has a long tradition of taking twelve-year-old schoolkids into the woods for a week of hands-on field science. Called Outdoor School, this program has taken kids out of their classrooms over the last six decades and mixed them with other kids from schools throughout the state. They learn collaboration and leadership skills along with lessons on soil, water, trees, and animals. Despite how incredibly successful this program has been, with proven positive effects on learning outcomes and dropout reduction, as school budgets have declined, Outdoor School has become an unaffordable extra. From a participation rate of close to 90%, today less than half of Oregon's sixth graders attend any program at all, usually a shorter and less impactful one.

I went to OFRI for their support for a campaign to restore Outdoor School funding for all schoolchildren in Oregon. Despite support from OFRI's director, I feared that the ideological gulf between the OFRI board and me might be too great to bridge. Here I was, a Portland liberal with a long history of working on environmental issues. There they were, rural, conservative business leaders dependent on exploiting natural resources. To prepare, I read their website carefully and reviewed their outreach and educational materials, seeking to find the underlying values rather than focusing on their message that cutting trees is good. (See TRY IT NOW #1 on the three Vs—Values, Value, and Voice.) The night before I was to make my ask, I joined them for dinner, listening carefully to their keynote speaker and, most keenly, to comments and questions from the audience. I had a drink in the bar afterward with some OFRI staff members, asking them about what they did and their backgrounds.

The next morning I sat in the audience during their board meeting. I heard them talk sincerely about their efforts to explain how the long-term success of their industry relied on cutting trees no faster than the trees could grow. How they were dealing with changing climate through planting many different species. How methods like clear-cutting were misunderstood by people unfamiliar with landscape-scale forest management. How proud they were of how they protected wildlife habitat and water quality. Clearly, they saw themselves as good stewards of the land.

Before I spoke, a request for funds by another organization was rejected, not even being seconded. This group had proposed developing a software app to help small woodland owners better manage their timber—an idea that had the support of the OFRI staff. Yet this organization regularly criticizes the timber industry over the impact of logging on salmon. It was seen as an enemy of the industry despite the usefulness of the proposal. I was worried about how they'd treat me.

I kept in mind what I had heard that morning and the previous night. Despite representing major corporations with considerable influence in Oregon and across the country, they felt attacked and misunderstood. There *were* many things they were doing to lessen damage while harvesting the forest, but most Oregonians paid little attention to the details. As one survey they funded showed, most of Oregon was a "drive-through" experience for urban dwellers, who see logging and especially clear-cuts destroying Oregon's beauty.

I was requesting funds to hold a series of meetings around Oregon. We wanted to meet with business, education, and community leaders to find out what they saw as the value of outdoor education in their communities. I thought of what I had heard: how the people at OFRI spoke of the values of stewardship, of providing jobs in rural communities, of a desire to be understood, and of their need to find a way to communicate with a population whose lives didn't depend on or interact with the woods like theirs did.

So that is what we talked about: how Outdoor School engaged young people at a critical time in their lives; how it gave them tools to understand their world, especially the connection between nature and natural resources; how it helped them become better citizens who could critically evaluate their choices and make more responsible decisions. I used their words to talk about my proposal—*stewardship*, *fact-based*, *hands-on*, *local knowledge*. And they got it. In addition to approving a $25,000 grant, they endorsed the project of restoring Outdoor School in Oregon. To have this group of powerful, conservative businesses agree to support raising taxes to restore Outdoor School was significant. As much or more so than getting the grant.

RECOGNIZING YOUR PLACE OF PRIVILEGE

Back in chapter 1, I spoke about recognizing my place of privilege within my community ecosystem. Now, this is for everyone reading this book. Every one of us is privileged. Admitting your privilege, whatever its source, is an important step toward being able to build trust and effective collaborations.

"What?" you might say, indignantly or in surprise. "I'm not (wealthy, male, white, Ivy League, straight, connected, charismatic, handsome, beautiful, talented—fill in the blank). How can I be privileged?" If you have the education to be able to read, you are already a minority of humanity, with billions either too poor to afford schooling or denied schooling because of their gender, social position, ethnicity, or politics. If you have food on the table at night, if you can walk your town's streets safely, if you aren't followed by security when entering a bank or shopping mall, you are privileged. This is not to say that you have the same privileges as someone who is wealthy, white, Ivy League, connected, charismatic, handsome, beautiful, and talented! We all bring our history to the table. Our backgrounds and life opportunities bestow us with privileges. Recognizing our privilege and how it affects the way we see the world is crucial if we want others to trust and work with us.

I had always thought of myself as an ordinary, "normal" guy. I worked hard (delivering newspapers from age eleven), studied with discipline in school, attended a state university, and followed the rules. I may have been normal for *my* community, but outside of that community I represented the privileged of society, and I was clueless about my privilege. What do I look like to others? Another old white guy. One who's had a fancy title and a position of power. Privileged, privileged, privileged! Only after I had worked with affordable housing activists and other advocates for the poor like the Urban League did I really understand how easy I had had it. As a white man, I could walk into any room and feel the right to be there. With my good education, I spoke in a way that was comfortable to decision makers. I could write in standard business English. I knew how to format a letter and what honorific to use. With my self-confidence from a life of privilege, I could call the mayor and expect to hear back. If I didn't hear back, I would have no compunction about calling back again and again until I got through. Although it's obvious to me now (and I will tell you soon about how my eyes were opened), many of my fellow activists, especially from minority or immigrant communities, experience American life quite differently. Their experiences told them a different story: You don't belong. You won't be listened to. You aren't one of us.

Your privilege can work against you, as well. Having power can make it harder to be open to new ideas. You may feel that you've *earned* the right to your opinions. You worked hard to get a good education, to rise to your social position, to earn your wealth, to make it through the school of hard knocks, or perhaps to win an election. Society reinforces our differences and sense of entitlement by bestowing titles or initials after our names. All this can go to our heads and make us expect people to listen to us—and make us shut down or get defensive when they ask *us* to hear *them*.

And, as part of the game of status, when we want to get support from those more privileged than us, we unconsciously check our own opinions at the door of the exclusive club to which they belong. This is hard-won knowledge, and, I confess, I did it myself. Especially when I was running for higher office, I'd find myself adjusting how I presented my ideas to fit the audience, often not challenging the powerful and wealthy, simply because they were powerful and wealthy—as I sought their support.

The more time you spend in leadership positions, the harder it is to keep your mind open. Continuing success requires being intentional about hearing and respecting other perspectives. In contrast to the American norm, in many traditions, elders listen more than they speak. They encourage others to explore their ideas without judging. They ask questions, such as "Why?" and "What would it look like if . . . ?" Sometimes I imagine that I am one of these elders. The image of a wise person in my head helps me step back from the moment, so I can assess whether I am reacting to my perceptions of the other and myself or whether I am really hearing the other person.

DON'T BE SILENCED BY STEREOTYPES

When the great science communicator Neil deGrasse Tyson earned his PhD in astrophysics from Columbia University in 1991, he was asked to give the convocation to his graduating class. He noted that at the time there were roughly four thousand astrophysicists living in the United States and that his graduation brought "the total number of African Americans among them to a paltry seven." He spoke openly of the challenges he faced: "In the perception of society . . . my academic failures are expected and my academic successes are attributed to others . . . To spend most of my life fighting these attitudes levies an emotional tax that is a form of intellectual emasculation. It is a tax that I would not wish upon my enemies."[3]

Research into the psychological effects of negative stereotypes shows that simply being reminded of one's relative status can cause poor performance at work, in sports, and in school. "Stereotype threat," as this effect is called, causes a drop in self-confidence that leads to the poorer performance that familiar stereotypes describe. For example, when asked to identify themselves by gender or race, women do worse on math tests and African American students earn lower grades—even white athletes' performance will falter when they are reminded of their race as the prevailing stereotype is that African Americans are the better athletes. It turns out

---

3. Yong. Ed. "Armor against Prejudice," *Scientific American*, June 2013.

that worrying itself reduces our ability to think and solve problems. When we worry about doing poorly because of our relative status, we do worse. Then we worry more, which leads to even poorer performance. It's a vicious and debilitating downward cycle.

Given this research, I wonder about how our effectiveness at work and success in life is affected even by well-meaning comments that highlight one's race, gender, or sexual orientation. When I compliment a woman on her dress or hairstyle, am I being polite or subtly reminding her of her gender—and the stereotypes about it—and thereby harming her performance? When we ask job applicants or survey takers to identify themselves by race, do we cause them to interview poorly? These are interesting questions that I can't answer, only something to be aware of and try to avoid.

It is reasonable to have doubts about our abilities. There is so much to know about how the world works. I regularly discover things I didn't know about my own area of expertise and even my long-term relationships. But stereotype threat is not about ignorance or a lack of skill. It is about how our *perceptions of ourselves*—not our actual capabilities—can affect our success. About whether we subconsciously limit our effectiveness below our potential. So how can we manage our subconscious sensitivity to social stereotypes so that we do our best despite them? In the context of leadership, how can we keep stereotypes from reducing our own and others' effectiveness?

Amazingly, simple exercises in personal affirmation can overcome our innate response to stereotyping. In one study, African American students who wrote these essays performed comparably to their white peers, while the African American students who didn't write these essays performed worse in the course.[4] Other research suggests that performance-busting anxiety can be relieved by explicitly acknowledging that everyone struggles at times and worries whether their ideas are worthwhile. Positive affirmations work.

---

4. Cohen, Geoffrey L. and Julio Garcia. "Social-Psychological Interventions: Solving the Scaling-Up Problem." *Scientific American*, Volume 308, Issue 6, May 2013.

TRY IT NOW #6

Overcoming Stereotype Impacts

Things you can do to overcome the negative impact of stereotypes:

1. Set aside time during a meeting or one-on-one discussion to have people share what they are struggling with. Often people don't see how hard others have to work to succeed or realize that others have doubts and challenges. From the outside we may see only competence. Understanding that others have difficulties—and find ways to overcome them—can inspire people to overcome their own.

2. Encourage people to share their successes and positive experiences out loud at regularly scheduled "celebrations" of your group's work, which can be during a regular staff meeting at "beer-thirty" on Friday afternoon. Share your own struggles, as well.

3. Here is another opportunity for using a journal for self-reflection and a reality check. Set aside time regularly to write down your thoughts about your life. Make sure to note the things that have gone well—tasks accomplished, good ideas you've thought of, et cetera. I keep a running list of tasks in a notebook, putting a little square next to each one. As I complete the task, I put an *X* in the box. Even this simple action gives me a sense of accomplishment and makes it easier to take on more.

4. Write down your top five strengths (generosity or creativity, for instance). Use one of the five strengths in a new and different way every day for a week. Research shows this can increase satisfaction and performance for the next six months!

5. Write down the good things. Again, research shows that people who take the time to write down things that went well and why they happened feel happier and more effective for up to six months after this simple exercise.

We depend on everyone doing his or her part well. Helping people do their best improves our chances of success. By doing these exercises, which reflect new research, our organizations and communities can help people overcome attitudes that reduce their effectiveness. Here's an example of how we used these ideas in a group I helped found, even though at the time we had no idea of the psychological basis for their power.

FROM THE TRENCHES

Overcoming Us-and-Them Thinking

In 1994, I was one of eight activists who organized the Coalition for a Livable Future (CLF). Our goal was to bring together, for the first time, all organizations that shared goals of making the Portland region more sustainable, no matter what issue they focused on. We knew that there were hundreds of advocates working on issues that touched on one of the three Es of sustainability—Equity, Environment, and Economy. But for the most part, these groups hadn't connected or worked with each other. The purpose of founding the CLF was to facilitate linkages as well as to bridge significant cultural gaps between the organizations. The initial founders included advocates for affordable housing, community development, conservation, alternative transportation, and smart land use. Despite a quiet beginning—our inaugural press conference was the day of the Northridge earthquake in California, and no media showed up—the group quickly grew to include most progressive groups in the region, attracting national attention for our inclusive, multi-issue organizing. Today, more than one hundred organizations are members.

We came together to influence policies throughout the Portland, Oregon, metropolitan area, taking advantage of the existence of a regional government, Metro. Voter passage of a citizen initiative required Metro to adopt a fifty-year vision for the region—and to adopt a Regional Framework Plan to guide implementation of this vision. Our bringing together so many diverse interests to focus on making the plan respond to community concerns bore fruit, getting many progressive policies adopted by the Metro Council. But what I found most exciting and of lasting value to my work were the methods we used to engage and energize these groups to work together in ways they had never done before.

Coalitions typically come together around one or a few common issues, existing only long enough to get action on these few issues and then disband. We hoped for more. We wanted to build something lasting and transformative. We hoped to build relationships of trust between people who hadn't worked together before and who often saw themselves on opposing sides of issues. We wanted to create the opportunity for people to see that they had a broad set of common interests.

The CLF brought together people from very different backgrounds of class and education. Imagine members of the League of Women Voters, made up of mostly upper-middle-class women, sitting down to lunch with immigrant rights workers. There were bearded environmentalists, African American rights advocates, bicycle geeks, and religious leaders of many faiths. One of the founders of the CLF, Tasha Harmon—executive director of an affordable housing group with years of experience in organizing—pushed us to focus first on developing personal relationships and deliberately set aside discussions about issues and policies until a later time. She had us share ways that our lives had been affected by each of the issues we were targeting. At the beginning of every general CLF meeting, we formed a big circle, all of us sitting next to someone we didn't know. Turning to that person, we'd talk about how issues had affected us personally. In a discussion of affordable housing, my soon-to-be-friend LeAnne told me that she had never thought about the cost of housing, as she was of the generation where women went straight from their parents' home to their husbands'. She had never paid rent. She had never worried about where she would sleep. She didn't even know how much her mortgage payment was. My most difficult time with housing costs was during the recession of the early '80s, when I worked odd jobs like dishwashing and had to live in a garage that cost me twenty-five dollars a month. Another woman told how she grew up keeping a knapsack by her bed, packed with clothes and a favorite toy, because she never knew when her mother would wake her and her sister in order to move out under the cover of darkness. Another time, people shared how they enjoyed nature with their families: Celeste remembered fishing at the local quarry for perch and crappie with her father. Some talked about big family picnics in the local park. Still others talked about long backpacking trips in the mountains and how they loved the solitude they found there.

The CLF grew in power, I believe, not because of our political savvy or expertise, but because we got to know each other as people first. As fellow humans—people with hopes and dreams—rather than as "the advocate for such and such" who sat across the room and only talked about his or her issue. In addition to forging bonds between people who hadn't worked together before and, in most cases, had never met, these exercises helped to reduce the friction that can occur when the conversation is too focused on actions and positions. Starting meetings this way built trust. We also avoided a common problem of a few people dominating discussion—particularly those privileged by society. United by the process of sharing our stories, we were able to propose and effectively advocate for sweeping new ideas to promote sustainability in our region. Whereas in chapter 2 there was a TRY IT NOW exercise that encouraged you, personally, to tell and hear stories—and write them down—now you want to work as a leader to get those you are organizing to share stories with each other. Here's an exercise to help you do just that.

TRY IT NOW #7

Sharing Stories to Build Trust

This is actually very simple and fun. You will learn so much about your community and make new friends, too!

Ask people to pair off with someone they don't already know well. If you want, you can count off by twos if people are shy about mingling. Give them a question that connects to the work you are doing in a personal way. What you are trying to do is get people to share something that affected them personally, not trade philosophies or talk abstractly. Here are a few ideas:

- If your issue is social justice, have people talk about being pulled over by a police officer. How often has it happened? What was the officer's attitude?

- If your issue is environmental, ask what people's best memory of nature was growing up. Was it an outing at a local park? Did their parents take them camping or fishing?

- If your issue is affordable housing: tell a story of how your life was affected by the cost of housing. (See the story of the founding of the Coalition for a Livable Future above.)

- Taking on a project in the neighborhood, school, or church? Tell each other what you felt like when someone did something for you in the past, such as volunteering in your classroom when you were young or helping you with a big project at your home. Why did you think this person did what they did? How does this affect your interest in volunteering?

- Dealing with a traffic problem, like cars going too fast? Share stories of how a car crash impacted your life. Most of us know someone who was killed or hurt in a car crash, and these stories make the danger of inattentive or thoughtless driving real rather than abstract.

DARE TO BE THE OTHER

Like fish swimming in the water, we are unaware of the culture we were raised and live in. We don't know we are wet, so to speak. What is it like to walk into a room full of people who don't look like you, talk like you, or act like you? To know you are seen as different by the others in the room, when they all seem to belong there? When it is clear that they know each other, share the same lingo, and look like they know what they are doing?

American society operates under the assumption that there is a "normal" way to behave. With our family and friends we share history and culture. We refer to the same television shows, newspapers, and books. Even if we are in intense disagreement over a particular issue, we share attitudes about how to argue, who should be listened to, and what is the proper way to conduct an argument, even. It's no surprise that "normal" often means white, middle-class behavior. Despite how much we share as humans, every culture has its own ways of ordering relations and making decisions. There really is no "normal" or universal code of behavior.

Our unconscious expectations often get in the way of our ability to build coalitions. I can't repeat this enough, especially as the organizations focused on issues I work on a lot—climate change, sustainability, urban revitalization—bemoan the lack of diversity of their members, activists, and boards. It isn't for lack of trying; most of these groups engage in diversity awareness trainings and bring in consultants to help them reach out to members of minority and immigrant communities. But they remain bewildered when their efforts fail to engage people of color or from different ethnic backgrounds.

One of my African American friends put it to me this way: It's as if all white people receive a secret decoder ring sometime early in their lives, which gives them the magical ability to ignore all the barriers African Americans face. All white people assume that African Americans already have the rights they are still fighting for today, such as voting and fair treatment by the justice system. Class, gender, and ethnic background put other groups at a similar disadvantage. Acknowledging the secret decoder ring on our own fingers allows us to help less privileged people to break the code and be more effective in their own struggles.

Why should this concern us if we are white, middle class, and educated? The United States has changed a lot in the past few decades. The idea of "minority" is becoming obsolete when it comes to talking about residents of the US. In the 2000s, California became the first state to have more than fifty percent of its population made up of people of non-European ancestry. Other states aren't far behind. We will work more and more with people who don't share our cultural and ethnic backgrounds. While overt discrimination is disappearing, nonwhite, less educated, and poorer communities still stand outside the system of power and still struggle for success. Four hundred years of European conquest and cultural dominance, as well as structural income inequality, still present barriers that prevent many people from prospering. These will never be overcome unless the white, educated, and privileged address them head-on in their own lives and in their organizations.

TRY IT NOW #8

Stranger in a Strange Land (but in Good Hands)

Here are some strategies I've found effective for improving how we relate to and connect with our fellow citizens in ways that are authentic and meaningful for all involved.

Take this on as a personal as well as an organizational challenge. Understanding the barriers to meaningful involvement by people of racial, class, or ethnic minorities is something that can only happen through direct, personal experience. Remember what it was like trying to join a club when you were a kid but didn't know the secret handshake or even where the clubhouse door was located? That's how I felt when I went to my first meetings of groups like the NAACP and the Asian Leadership Network. Feeling "different" made me self-conscious. I thought people were looking at me funny. (They were; I was a new face, and they wanted to make sure to welcome me!) I was unsure of myself, not knowing the proper etiquette regarding who spoke when. I didn't understand that when people spoke loudly at the NAACP meeting, they weren't angry. Or how the Asian leaders seemed to arrive at decisions without anyone seeming to talk very much. I was unprepared for how self-conscious I felt as the only white guy in the room. A lesson in humility but also a challenge.

Make yourself a list of the groups you would like to build coalitions with and places or organizations you might have been avoiding because of their "otherness" or your reluctance to be the stranger. This could be something as simple as a coffee shop in a different neighborhood. Remember, you are not going to be a tourist and "watch the natives" at, say, a Puerto Rican poetry slam, a lesbian bookstore, or an African American café. You're there to engage.

ORGANIZATION/ PLACE/EVENT	PURPOSE OF ENGAGEMENT	CONTACT PERSON OR "LOCAL GUIDE"

FROM THE TRENCHES

Get Some Help

I wasn't going to these groups to be a tourist; I was hoping to be able to understand their concerns and issues because I was *their* elected representative. I wanted to get their help in moving forward with an agenda we would all benefit from. I knew that if I couldn't forge effective alliances with them, I would be less successful in my role. I would fail those I had pledged to represent. After a series of these unsuccessful and uncomfortable experiences, I knew I needed some help.

My African American friends suggested that I attend a class offered by a local group called Uniting to Understand Racism.[5] This group worked mostly with eighth-grade students in the public schools as part of a community effort to reduce racial tension and gang violence. Their goal was to help minority and immigrant students feel more comfortable in the school setting so they would remain in school rather than drop out. In their workshops for adults, they sought to get people to recognize underlying cultural assumptions that trip up even well-meaning people and make them less effective with people of other cultures. For me, this meant understanding the privilege I enjoyed as an educated white male.

---

5. http://resolutionsnorthwest.org

As I told you before, I had been uncomfortable sitting in the back of a room of people who looked different from me. Now imagine my discomfort when I was the center of attention! In our particular group, I was the only white American male and, boy, did they let me have it! I found myself backpedaling away from responsibility for three hundred years of slavery and misogyny. But, I protested, my ancestors didn't even immigrate to this country until after the Civil War and slavery ended. I considered myself a feminist, as well. But that isn't the point, they answered back. They told me that by virtue of my skin color, gender, and socioeconomic background, my experience of the world was qualitatively different from theirs. If I didn't recognize this, I could never build trusting relationships and strong alliances with their communities. I didn't have to renounce who I was, but I did need to see both my privilege and the ways in which their lives were vastly different from mine.

The class lasted eight weeks. It took me to the fourth week before I stopped defending myself and started to realize what it meant to be the "other" in the room. In this group, for the first time, *I* was the one who didn't understand subconscious social cues shared by people of a similar background. I was the one who had to change and conform to someone else's cultural expectations—to be who I wasn't— in order to be "seen." I came to realize how courageous people of color, women, immigrants, or low-income people must be to walk into a room full of white males, who still hold most power in business and government. I saw how many cultural nuances they have to juggle while trying to be heard, and I realized they had to perform this juggling act without losing their own sense of authenticity.

RESOURCES FOR ENGAGING WITH THE "OTHER"

First of all, congratulations. If you are reading this section, you are brave enough to face one of the most challenging and divisive issues in US society. You will be overwhelmed. And there is little you can do to prepare for the emotions that discussing racism, inequality, and injustice will bring up in any group: denial, anger, disbelief, frustration. But there is help out there. Like the group I worked with in Portland, all across the country there are people and organizations that will help you and your organization understand and develop strategies to counter the damage that racism has done to our society. What follows is a list of resources, but I also recommend looking for help in your community, as this is not an abstract exercise best done alone, by reading. Good luck.

Organizations, many of which provide training:

- Western States Center: www.westernstatescenter.org
- Center for Diversity and the Environment: www.cdeinspires.org
- Racial Equity Institute: rei.racialequityinstitute.org

Books:

- A free download of a resource book for dealing with racism in organizations and in society from a group I greatly respect: www.westernstatescenter.org/tools.../Dismantling%20Racism/download
- An extensive bibliography on works on racism and white privilege: http://www.wpcr-boston.org/index_files/page0006.htm

Websites:

- Simon Tam, "Give Racism a Chance": http://youtu.be/J0ruIuwb8vw
- The Race Project of the American Anthropological Association: http://understandingrace.org/home.html
- Youth Helping to End Racism: www.anti-racismonline.org
- Race: The Power of an Illusion: https://www.pbs.org/race/000_General/000_00-Home.htm
- Showing Up for Racial Justice: http://www.showingupforracialjustice.org

REWRITING THE RULES FOR EVERYONE

America's dominant culture is white, middle class, and educated. We—all of us, no matter what our history or background—are expected to conform to its norms and values. These norms and values may be self-evident and "natural" to the members of that culture but are often mysterious barriers to many Americans.

Let's look at government meetings as an example. Decisions are made there that determine the future of your community, your home. Yet most government meetings are scheduled during the day, when most people can't take off work. The lobbyist or the executive can make it to push their interest, though. Or, if meetings are held at night, it is rare for childcare or food to be provided. The meetings are held in government offices, most likely downtown, not in the community, with security screenings, paid parking, and intimidating procedures. Most meetings are still run as if we are subjects petitioning our rulers for favors. Judgment is passed down from on high, with deference given to those who speak in a certain way or represent certain interests (business concerns foremost among them). Details may differ, but much public engagement today still reflects and reinforces an ancient and feudal culture of privilege. Sure, our "rulers" are now people we elect, but they still sit up above us on a dais and follow rules drafted centuries ago to empower insiders.

These rules, such as Robert's Rules of Order, used by most public bodies in the US, favor form over content, giving knowledgeable insiders the means to steer decision-making in their favor. It is not just government that is failing to create better ways for all Americans to access their government—many social movements still shut out those from other cultures and races by failing to examine how they replicate the behavior of the dominant culture in their organizations, how they frame their message, and who they reach out to. Witness the struggle of mainstream environmental groups to attract people of color. Love of nature and getting out of doors is certainly not restricted to white people, but that's the conclusion you would come to if you looked at membership and board makeup of most environmental groups.

Why should those in power care? We are in a crisis in America. People have stopped engaging—voting levels are down, and it's hard to get anyone to show up to a meeting or answer a poll—even on important decisions affecting them directly. Disengagement leads to cynicism, division, and distrust, undermining the social cohesion, the "we are all in this together" feeling we will need to resolve the challenges we face. In a country made up of citizens from many diverse cultures and histories, developing ways to engage all people is a matter of survival. We need new approaches to capitalize on the benefits of this incredible richness. It is time to stop asking people to conform to a single model of engagement. We need to engage and mobilize all citizens. And that will require fundamental changes in what leaders, like you (yes, you!) demand of their organizations and of themselves.

CHAPTER 3 BLUEPRINT FOR CHANGE

As we've learned in this chapter—and as I've learned through long experience—change rarely comes from the efforts of a lone person but almost always through group effort. Leaders count—don't get me wrong. And the whole premise of this book is to help you become a better leader. But, no matter how great your qualifications for leadership, you won't get squat done without getting buy-in from others, be they volunteers, community members, or employees. In this part of our journey, you have learned how to:

- Keep from reinventing the wheel by finding others working on your cause (locally and nationally).
- Survive your first meeting and make it a great success.
- Find the natural leaders in the room.
- Avoid letting the furniture run (or ruin) the meeting.
- Find a local guide who will give you an insider's perspective.
- Deal with haters.
- Step into the shoes of the "other" and gain new perspectives.

- Avoid the dangers of stereotyping and being stereotyped.
- Get help to understand the world from the perspective of other racial, ethnic, and socioeconomic groups.
- Use your knowledge of cultural richness to create openings for greater engagement.

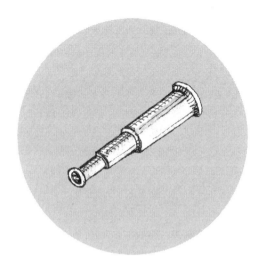

CHAPTER 4

CONFRONTING KEY CHALLENGES OF THE ACTIVIST LIFE

"What makes a king out of a slave? Courage.

What makes the flag on the mast to wave? Courage.

What makes the elephant charge his tusk in the misty mist

or the dusky dusk?

What makes the muskrat guard his musk? Courage.

What makes the sphinx the seventh wonder? Courage.

What makes the dawn come up like thunder?! Courage."

—*The Cowardly Lion in* The Wizard of Oz

In this chapter you will find a list of common challenges you will face as you work to make the world a better place.

- How to manage your (and others') time effectively.
- How to motivate volunteers to give their time and energy again and again.
- How to get others to fund your cause.
- How to avoid burnout.

- How to learn and benefit from failure.

No one can give you definitive answers for how to overcome these and other challenges; there isn't space in this small book for more than getting you started. But there *are* ways to prepare yourself to deal with whatever comes up. And don't forget what we went over in earlier chapters about being clear on your values and your role in the world—knowing yourself and how to ask others for help will always be critical ingredients of success, whatever you are doing.

CHALLENGE #1

Motivating People to Rally to Your Cause

On my way to my office one day I passed by the Metro Council chambers, usually empty in the morning. But that day there was a crowd. I wandered in to see what was up. Specialists in invasive-species removal were talking about their efforts to eliminate these in natural areas and parks. They were sharing their successes as well as the frustrations of dealing with the challenge of removing weeds like English ivy, holly, Scotch broom, and others that outcompete native species and severely damage native ecosystems. I decided to listen in for just a bit.

The first speaker was a volunteer coordinator at Tryon Creek State Park, the only state park inside the urban area of Portland. Surrounded by urban development, park managers struggle to control nonnative plants that invade from nearby yards. With tight budgets and big weed problems, it's impossible to make much of a dent in the invasive-plant problem with just staff; volunteers are critical to any chance of success. In contrast to the other speakers that day, who focused on particular plant species and control strategies, she talked about motivating volunteers, focusing in particular on understanding why people would give their time for such difficult tasks as pulling tenacious weeds. This is hard, dirty, repetitive, and seemingly endless work. So how do you get people to give up Saturday upon Saturday to do this? She described strategies from her previous career in marketing used to persuade people to buy stuff. Could the same psychological motivators that sell computers and sneakers motivate volunteers to pull weeds?

She laid out a three-point description of the decision-making process someone might go through when considering whether to commit to a volunteer gig—a process not so different from the one we go through when we consider making a major purchase.

- Can I do it? (Am I physically able? Does it fit in my schedule? Can I get to the location?)
- Are others in my peer group doing similar things? (In other words, by doing this, will I be seen as a weirdo or part of the in-crowd?)
- If a lot of us do this thing, will it make a significant difference? (Even if it seems overwhelming to me alone, by working with others, can we succeed?)

When Barack Obama first ran for president, he used this strategy to shape his message. Consider his campaign's slogan, "Yes We Can." It captures all three points above: the possibility of individual action, the fun and excitement of being part of a movement, and the ability to succeed if people work together. The United Farm Workers under Cesar Chavez actually used this same slogan decades ago during their struggle to win higher wages and improve working conditions for farm workers in California. ("*Si Se Puede*" translates as "Yes, We Can.")

Now, consider how you talk about your own work. How might you use these three motivation factors to rally others to work for your cause—whether you need people to pull weeds, serve on your board, donate money, or get out the vote?

TRY IT NOW #9

Test Your Motivational Power

Face it: getting people to give their time and energy can be tough. That's why people get paid to work! Money motivates! But most community projects rely on people voluntarily giving up time for leisure or spending with their families. Many things that need to happen to achieve your goals are dull, difficult, and repetitive—stuffing envelopes, knocking on doors, entering data into a database. How you talk about the work that needs to be done can either inspire or turn off potential volunteers. Use the following technique to change people's response from "not for me" to "yes we can!"

What are the "To Dos"—the tasks—you need help with to realize your goal? Do they meet the three requirements described above that get people excited and willing to get involved? Individual efficacy, peer acceptance, and group efficacy. Do you describe the tasks in ways that people can easily understand how their effort contributes to the desired outcome? For each task, whether petitioning or mural painting, use the following scheme to test the motivational strength of your message before you present your "To Dos" to your potential volunteers.

MOTIVATIONAL FACTOR	How Program/Project Meets Their Needs
INDIVIDUAL EFFICACY	Can a volunteer do this task? (Some tasks, like ivy pulling, are tedious and somewhat physically demanding.) Match the task to the skills of the person!
PEER ACCEPTANCE	Can you get a group like the Boy Scouts or college service clubs to come out together and help you with this task? Start the day by having people introduce themselves and say why they are there. Yes, I am part of a larger whole!
GROUP EFFICACY	What is the cumulative impact of working together, e.g., X number of acres that are ivy-free? At the end of the day, can people step back and see how much they accomplished?

MOTIVATIONAL FACTOR	
INDIVIDUAL EFFICACY	
PEER ACCEPTANCE	
GROUP EFFICACY	

We all seek meaning in our lives. What better way to give people meaning than to give them something to do where their efforts make a real difference and they can see that difference? By presenting the work in ways that speak to the basic human need to be needed, you will be able to talk about your work more effectively, enabling you to engage and recruit even more people to help. By presenting your work in this way, you will make what is self-evident to you more accessible to others. Give it a try!

CHALLENGE #2

Rounding Up, and Keeping, Your Volunteers

Even if your volunteers are motivated and passionate about your cause, you should be thinking always of how to keep their excitement and commitment high so that they will continue to show up at meetings, protests, work parties, and other events. What gets people to come back, to NOT push the snooze button on days they said they would show up? Consider this list a starting point.

- Always get commitments in writing from volunteers. You can do this on a general sign-up list or on a separate sign-up list for specific duties (ask a volunteer to be the lead for each duty).

- Have volunteer job descriptions outlining what is expected of the volunteer and what the volunteer can expect of the group.

- Call volunteers personally. Let them know they matter.

- Always provide something to eat and drink at meetings. Low cost but healthy snacks are fine. Food is magical and also an important part of human bonding.

- Switch times of meetings so they are not always during the workday (alternate early morning meetings with evening meetings). Better yet, survey the group as to the best meeting times. Make it convenient and easy for *them*.

- Don't waste people's time. So often I've shown up to volunteer and no one has given me a task to do, or I stand around waiting for organizers to get organized, so I feel like my time has been wasted (only ask for the number of volunteers you need and assign specific tasks for each event).

- Provide legal aid numbers and other support if you are asking volunteers to participate in a protest.

- Volunteers from middle school through college age are motivated by the word "intern." This is something they can put on college or job applications.

- Retiring baby boomers are a huge, untapped resource, and they are skilled and experienced. For older volunteers, who may want to use their skills or learn new ones, offer real work to do (writing your press releases, computer programming, and so on).

- Recognize people's contributions. Give them the credit they deserve—publicly and frequently. Simple and inexpensive awards or certificates should be personalized. A handwritten thank-you note can be tremendously moving as well as motivating.

CHALLENGE #3

Finding Time to Be a Leader
(You Can't Do Everything!)

I used to feel guilty when I went for a hike or read a good novel, thinking that such diversions were self-indulgent when there was so much wrong in the world that needed fixing. The world was going to hell, and I was going for a hike? The media loves stories of saintly activists like Mother Teresa or ascetic activists like Ralph Nader, giving us an image of activism impossible to imagine for ourselves. Of course we all want to do good. But we also want to live good lives. We want to fall in love, laugh, enjoy good food, raise a family. Too often, the way activists are portrayed, it seems that you have to sacrifice yourself in order to do good for others.

Just as we need to find the right balance between work and personal life, the same quandary arises when you are faced with balancing your desire to say yes to everything and your need to keep up your spirit through love, friendship, and finding joy in the world. This is true when someone asks you to volunteer or when you see a problem you think you want to help solve.

Luckily, being active doesn't have to mean giving up family, work, and fun. Look around your community; you will see many people doing good works—at their place of worship, with a neighborhood association, or in their kid's school. Most wouldn't say they are "activists," yet they are making positive change happen and improving lives by their actions. They are activists in my book.

Finding balance is good for you but also good for causes you care about. Balance allows you to keep on contributing throughout your life. Think of it as personal sustainability. Activism and leadership can be part of your life, not something apart from it. Make a living. Be a good spouse, parent, and coworker. Make music, plant a garden, walk on the beach. Enjoy life.

Over time, I have come up with some rules of thumb to help me keep a schedule and level of commitment that's good for my family and me. One was limiting myself to two evening meetings a week—unless something really, really important came up ;).

TIME MANAGEMENT FOR ACTIVISTS

Try it now #10–12

Thinking about your commitments and interest level early on in your involvement on any issue will help you use your time more effectively and strategically. It also reduces the likelihood that you will overpromise and underdeliver, actions that are hard on those you work with and that cast doubt on your credibility and effectiveness.

Here is a set of TRY IT NOW exercises that can help you make better choices in how you use your time. The goal is to be strategic: investing a very precious commodity in the most effective manner. Read through them all first and pick one (or more) that you think will be useful to you in figuring out how to prioritize your time.

TRY IT NOW #10

My Day

Make a list of what you do in a typical day and when and for how long each activity takes place. Here's what my life was like when I was a young parent:

ACTIVITY	TIME	THOUGHTS ON HOW I SPENT MY TIME
Wake up, coffee, newspaper	6:00–7:00	Quiet time, get my thoughts together about the day
Make breakfast, get kids to school	7:00–8:00	Shared with partner: a good thing!
Commute	8:00–8:30	On a good day!
Work	8:30–5:00ish	Focus on the tasks at hand and on others. Do it well!
Commute	5:00ish–5:30	At least I could ride my bike
Go for a run	5:30–6:30	Maybe twice a week?
Homework help, dinner	6:30–8:00	Again, good time with family
Downtime! Catch up with partner, prepare for next day at work	8:00–10:00	Wish I could have gotten all the tests graded at school
My time!	10:00–11:00	Read a book, watch TV
Sleep	11:00–6:00	At last!

With this schedule, it was hard to be much of an activist. My partner served on the neighborhood association board, which met only once a month. I was on the board of a community group promoting alternative energy, a small commitment of time. We made donations to causes we cared about. Some weekends we volunteered with local groups—planting trees or fixing up bikes for low-income families, taking our kids along to share the rewards that come with giving to others. We weren't huge activists by a long shot. The kids became middle schoolers, then high schoolers. They required a different kind of attention as their lives became busier and more independent of ours. (We always made sure to eat dinner together.) As our boys needed less of our time, we could recalibrate our civic engagement. I had time to volunteer with a new nonprofit organization that I ended up working for.

What's your list look like?

ACTIVITY	TIME	THOUGHTS ON HOW I SPENT MY TIME

TRY IT NOW #11

My Priorities

Make a list of what you'd like to do more of and what you'd like to do less of. For me, it looked like this:

MORE	LESS
Get to know my neighbors.	Commute less, find a job closer to home.
Something to do, like a hobby or activity that would help me relax.	Buy less, recycle more.
More time with kids and spouse.	Reduce time spent on chores by getting kids to help more.
Involvement with issues I care about.	Cleaning the house! (Get the kids to help.)

What's your list look like?

MORE	LESS

TRY IT NOW #12

My Delegation Skills

Part of good parenting is giving your kids ways they can help out around the house. Chores help them learn life skills like honoring commitments, having a sense of duty, and feeling the pride that comes from doing a task well. Do you give the same opportunity to your employees or volunteers? Numerous studies have shown that what inspires people—far more than financial incentives—is feeling that *their contributions make a difference.* Don't be shy about sharing the load with others—people want the responsibility! Can you let go of key tasks and responsibilities?

Questions to help you delegate effectively:

1. What needs to be done?
2. What is the time frame for completing these tasks?
3. How much time should each task take?
4. What skills are needed to complete the task? Are there special tools, e.g., a database, a computer, or mailing lists, needed to do the task?
5. What does the doer need to know in order to successfully complete the task?
6. What do you need to know about a person to feel comfortable in delegating a task to them?
7. Can you come up with a short description of the task that helps a volunteer or staff person understand what they will be expected to do?

Too often, we keep all this information in our heads and wonder why people don't just jump in and take on the work. Effective leaders share their vision as well as the steps they think it will take to get there. They also are open to hearing others' ideas. Listening is critical, especially if you are working with volunteers. By asking people about their skills, knowledge, and interests, you will be able to figure out with them how best to utilize them. It can be tough to let go of what we think are things that only we can do right. Yet I've found that, just like asking my kids to take responsibility for keeping the house clean, when I've asked others to share responsibility for achieving our goals, my work is made easier and the results are usually superior. You just get more done with more hands helping. And the pride people have in doing it themselves primes them for taking on bigger tasks.

A FINAL NOTE ON TIME MANAGEMENT

Remember these two important things:
life is short and you have time.

Old advice that we too often forget. Most religions and philosophies remind us to take the long view. It's much healthier. The average American lives into their late seventies. The first twenty years of your life are about growing up, gaining understanding of yourself and the world. The next forty years or so are typically devoted to work and family, with weekends and evenings available for community work. If you have kids, they eventually move on to their own lives when you are somewhere in your forties or fifties. Hopefully your life is less harried now and you are less worried about money. You will have time and experience to share with your community. In Latin countries they call this the "third age." I like that way of looking at getting older!

If you are working furiously to support your family, you may not have the time or energy to be in the heart of the struggle, so don't beat yourself up about it. Give what you can. It may be money, encouragement, or advice. Your role in your community will change as your life changes. Periodically reassess your commitments using the exercises in TRY IT NOW #10 and #11 in order to use your energies and interest well throughout your life.

CHALLENGE #4

Finding Funding

You can find many books on this subject detailing how to write grants, cultivate big donors, and recruit and retain supporters. Whether you are already running an organization or just starting one up, there are two things I want to make sure you think of that aren't addressed enough in the fund-raising literature: recruiting a dedicated core of supporters and not losing sight of your goal or control of your project in the fund-raising process.

Clarity about what you are doing is as critical to fund-raising as it is to all your activities. You are asking people to invest in your vision, and you owe it to them to have a clear idea of the problem you hope to solve and how you are going to do it. A great resource for help in developing the *how* is SCORE, a volunteer corps of retired executives. These retired execs helped a friend of mine, who founded an environmental nonprofit, write her business plan, hone her mission statement, and market her group to funders. It's a wonderful, absolutely free resource. They can help you craft a mission statement and maybe even a business plan before you start looking for funding.

So where do you find the money? When I first began running for office, I got this advice: ask ten of your friends for $100 apiece for your campaign. How many of them said yes, along with their enthusiasm or lack of it, would let me know immediately whether I had a chance as a candidate. Thankfully, everyone I asked said yes right away, launching my political career. Asking your close friends and colleagues to support a project you are thinking of launching is a good way for you to test the idea. It will also tell you how well you are able to communicate why it is important as well as how plausible your strategy is.

Then, ask *their* friends. If your close friends buy in, ask them to give you the names and contact information of ten of their friends and colleagues. Ask your friends if you can use them as references when calling. This will open up a lot of doors for you. Just by doing this you will already have one hundred possible donors! Think of fund-raising as a ripple on a pond, radiating out through society, gaining you more friends and supporters at each step. The amount of work—and the return you get—will inevitably decline as the circles widen. At some point, you will call people instead of meeting each one personally, then send out e-blasts and letters instead of calling, and so on. More advanced fund-raising is a science of combing through lists, email appeals, and special events. But never, and I mean never, neglect those closest to you who gave you your start and who will be your most loyal supporters. They are your core, your base, and they are invaluable.

Grow your base of support. A basic rule of fund-raising is that people will give money (and time) only if asked. Sure, some may say no, but people will never, ever say yes unless they are asked. Can you ask too much? When will your friends start to avoid you at parties or stop answering your calls? Hopefully, never. But be thoughtful about how much you go back to the same sources. You can avoid overdoing it by cultivating new supporters and new sources of funding.

- Prominently display a "donate" button on your website.
- Include donation links in email updates.
- Set aside time every week for calls to potential donors.
- Have your staff and board or other volunteers include fund-raising in their job descriptions.[6]
- Look for mission-related business opportunities.[7]
- Finally, offer your longtime supporters other ways to help, aside from writing a check or filling one particular role. Will they make a few phone calls on your behalf to potential supporters? Will they consider putting your organization in their will, ask if their employer has a matching grant

6. On joining the board of the Oregon Environmental Council, I signed an agreement that includes a commitment to raise $4,000 a year, either through a personal donation or through fund-raising; this is something to consider as you create your community brain trust or board of advisors we mentioned in chapter 2.
7. Free Geek is a Portland nonprofit that accepts unneeded computers from individuals and refurbishes them to give to low-income people and schools. In addition to charging a handling fee, volunteers salvage valuable components of unusable computers for resale and recycling, covering the cost of operating this service.

program, organize a house party or coffee at their workplace or place of worship to introduce you to new people? People like to be helpful, remember, but they also like to do something new once in a while!

THE THREE MAJOR SOURCES OF FUNDING

When you have bigger ideas than you can cover with small donations and volunteer effort, there are three major sources of money: individuals, corporations, and foundations.[8] Of the three, individual donors give much more, their donations come with fewer strings, and they can respond much faster to appeals. Finding supporters with means is the most difficult part of reaching individual donors. Sometimes they will come to you—a surprise donation of a much bigger sum than usual might show up, but finding, asking, and retaining major (however you define *major*) donors needs to be methodical.

Corporations look for opportunities to look good: sponsoring a public event or buying a table at a fund-raising dinner allows them to get their name out and associated with a good cause. Asking a foundation for a grant can be deceptively easy—they publish clear guidelines, usually have staff that can answer questions, and control a huge amount of money dedicated to civic purposes, but as a percentage of support for nonprofits, foundations give much less than individuals.

HUNTING AND CAPTURING MAJOR DONORS

Call this a research project or a hunt. People with money and interest *are* out there. You first have to find them, understand their interests, make contact with them, and

---

8. Governments can also be funders, mainly through contracts with social service providers. Sometimes they will fund a limited set of very specific projects meeting a particular need. The added complexity of satisfying government accountability rules and restrictions on advocacy makes government a much more difficult funding partner. In my experience, advocacy groups that get government support usually lose their edge.

know how much to ask for, and *then* make your case in a way that connects your work with their interests.

- **Finding potential major donors:** Your own membership and mailing lists are the first places to look. Many times people with resources will spontaneously make a contribution to causes in which they are interested. Short of a surprise multithousand-dollar gift, how do you know that your donors are capable of giving more? Here's where the hunt begins. I collect the annual reports of other nonprofit groups in my community. Contributors are often listed by how much they have given. I'd compare their list of donors with my membership list. If a person was listed as giving a big gift to this other group and gave to mine as well, I could assume that they were capable of giving a larger gift to mine. Don't just look at other groups like yours—look at museums, community foundations, and the United Way, as well as other community groups. Other good sources of information on big givers in your community are political contribution and expenditure reports, usually available from the secretary of state or state elections division.

- **Understanding their interests:** Just because someone gave $50 million to cancer research at the local university doesn't mean they'll write a big check for your group. Your job is not just to find people with money, but to find people who share your concerns. If someone has given big to another organization like yours, chances are they would be open to a request from you. Likewise, if they gave a contribution to a politician who ran on a platform of open government or police reform, and your group is working on these issues, you have a natural connection. Again, this is where research is important.

- **Making contact:** A community is made up of networks. Your current supporters are your best help in prioritizing who to ask. Sit down with your board, staff, and volunteers and go over the lists you've put together. Who do they know? Who do they work with? Who do their spouses work with or know? Do their kids go to the same school as people on the list? Do they work out at the same club? Donate to the same groups? Ask if you can use their names to get an appointment or call time with the potential donor. Better yet, ask if they will make the call themselves, either with you or on their own.

- **Determining what to ask for:** This can be a hard call, especially if this is the first time you've made contact with this person and they are unfamiliar with your group. People give large amounts out of loyalty for a particular leader or cause built up over time or because of a deep emotional connection. You can judge what their usual giving level is from the public reports, but you may also just ask them. But before you do this, you have to show them the value of what you are doing.

- **Making your case and connecting to their interests:** People give to causes they think are important AND to groups that are effective. People who give a lot get asked a lot. Be prepared. Use what I've written about earlier in this book to be clear on the problem you are trying to solve, your methods and why you think they are the most effective, how you are going to succeed, who else is on board (peer pressure is important to everyone), and what your need is. Your three Vs, your elevator speech, your outcomes, your budget—all are important to share.

- **Caring for and feeding donors:** Think of these people as volunteers, giving their money instead of their time. They require similar attention. Keep them informed of your work. Make personal contact with them on a regular basis, and not always to ask for money. One group that I donate to has their board members call major donors at least once a year just to say thank you (a voice-mail message works fine for this). Invite them to events. Ask about their families.

GETTING BUCKS FROM BUSINESS

Local businesses give out lots of money in their communities. Bigger corporations, like utilities and banks, often have foundations that give grants, but they also have marketing and public relations budgets that can be less formal and easier to access. Getting items for raffles and silent auctions is a way to get smaller businesses to support your group, but their giving tends to be limited, often to products or services they sell rather than cash. Then you have to go through the extra work of putting on an event to get people to bid on the donated items. Smaller businesses will give to what the owner or employees care about while bigger businesses are usually "buying" good will through their giving and are wary of what they see as political or advocacy groups. Now, sometimes a big company is supportive of an issue; for example, PGE, a large electric utility in the West, gives to projects to weatherize the homes of low-income people, to plant trees to absorb carbon dioxide, and to promote sustainability in general. This helps their image, of course, since their coal-fired power plants are some of the biggest polluters in the region. Understanding how corporate interests and yours line up—or don't—will help you be more successful in making an ask or save you the time if either party would feel that a contribution would compromise their position. Connect to smaller business owners through your networks—even if the only connection is that someone on your board or staff uses that business—say, shops at that store or has their taxes done by that accountant. Larger corporations have community or public affairs offices you can call and ask to sit down with to find out how your project might fit their interests.

GETTING FUNDS FROM FOUNDATIONS

"I know—let's write a grant!" How many times have you heard that one? Despite how much money is sitting in their accounts, foundations only have to give out a measly 5% of their holdings every year. Most grant requests are unsuccessful. Grants to fund advocacy are particularly hard to get. Just a warning: writing grants can seem so much easier than doing the work of making cold calls to people you don't know, many of whom will politely—or not so politely—decline to help. But grant writing takes time and practice to do well. In addition, many new activists make the mistake of writing a grant request without making contact with the trustees or staff of the foundation. Ask for an appointment to give your elevator speech, emphasizing your analysis of the problem, your strategy for fixing it, and your particular strengths that will make it likely for you to succeed. Ask them how they see your ideas fitting in with their vision and understanding of the dynamics in the community. Can they suggest other foundations, or individuals for that matter, that are concerned about this issue? Like corporations, the *people* at foundations are concerned about whether they will be seen as supporting a "winner." They don't like to stick their necks out. On the flip side, they are *people* who care about their community and may share your particular concerns, as well.

If I haven't scared you off of seeking funds from foundations, here are a few suggestions on where to start. There are great searchable databases available on the Web for free today that make the process of finding foundations that may share your interests much easier. One is the Foundation Center (http://www.foundationcenter.org). There is also a national network of progressive foundations that will fund advocacy. While the national office shut down in 2012, their local funds can still be located through http://fex.org/memberfoundations. They don't operate in all states but can be a source of good information for those working on social justice issues.

CHALLENGE #5

Keeping Focused on Your Goal

Because firing people and cutting back on activities are difficult, sometimes we will do things to raise money that undercut our effectiveness or independence. Two of the most common are pursuing grants even if the funds are restricted to activities tangential to the core mission and becoming overreliant on one source of funding—a specific individual, foundation, or government body—while neglecting to maintain strong grassroots fund-raising efforts. Sometimes well-meaning people in foundations or governments will offer to partner with your organization, offering funds to operate or establish programs on their behalf. In my experience, many organizations in this situation get distracted from their core mission, especially if advocacy is a key strategy. For my master's thesis, I interviewed ten people with combined experience running nonprofits of over two hundred years. Put in a few words, their conclusion was that becoming dependent on foundation or government grants inevitably ends up in converting advocates into dependent service providers. Advocates for public investment in housing were enticed with grants to start homeless shelters or manage public housing, getting diverted from advocating for longer-term solutions. Foundations by nature are conservative (after all, they serve to protect wealth), funding direct service or capital but rarely advocacy.

Avoiding this danger: Many nonprofit organizations get the opportunity to earn some money by providing services on contract with governments or foundations. While a growing budget can seem like a good thing, these relationships put pressure on the nonprofit to moderate its advocacy in order to keep these lucrative contracts or avoid offending partners. Deliberate or self-imposed muzzling isn't the only risk: the disruption that comes from potential loss of a major part of your funding stream is to be avoided at all costs because such a loss can permanently damage an organization, forcing the layoff of key personnel, discouraging active volunteers and board members, and making potential donors wary.

The Center for Intercultural Organizing (CIO), an immigrant rights group that I serve on the board of lost a major part of its income when a private foundation hired a new director who decided to change their funding priorities. Bang! Overnight, the CIO lost 40% of its funding, resulting in major pay cuts for key staff and forced layoffs. It was a wake-up call for the executive director, who immediately launched the CIO's first membership drive and formed its first fund-raising committee. He experienced the danger of relying on any one source of funding and the value of having a strong base of grassroots funding—many small donations from many people—as a more reliable and sustainable source of support for CIO's mission of advocacy.

CHALLENGE #6

Avoiding Burnout

Being a leader is tough work. Rewarding to be sure, but tough work nonetheless. How do people do it year after year? Have some leaders discovered the secret Fountain of Youth? Being excited about the next thing to come along helps (see the next section). Making significant change happen or completing an ambitious project takes time and persistence. The resistance to change is strong and not just from those who benefit from current inequities. It takes a lot for most people to get past "if it ain't broke (too badly), don't fix it." In this business, day in and day out, you do the same thing with the occasional win.

Let's go back to some of the earlier practices I wrote about on finding balance in your personal life and apply them to your worklife.

1. Take time to recognize that you are only human. You have obligations to your loved one, your family, and yourself. Be honest about how much you can do (see Finding Time to Be a Leader, Time Management for Activists).

2. Remember the Stoics' lesson that there are things we can change, things we can influence, and things we must accept. Focus where you have the ability to make a difference, and don't beat yourself up over what you are powerless to change.

3. Enjoy life! Celebrate wins. Celebrate the difference you have made in the world. These are the legacies you pass on to the next generation! I thank you for your work!

4. Be a good friend as well as leader. Treat yourself and your colleagues with respect, compassion, and understanding.

Research shows that we can expect to be productive for only about six hours of every workday. We are able to concentrate for about ninety minutes at most at a stretch, with about twenty minutes needed to rest and get ready for the next burst of productivity. Slaving away at your desk might look like dedication but won't gain you much, if it doesn't actually diminish your effectiveness. Too often we remain at our desks, drinking carry-out coffee and eating lunch by ourselves, hunched over a keyboard. As a leader, you can take advantage of our need to recharge and make work all the more fun for your group as well as improve productivity by synchronizing meetings and breaks so people can socialize and have the time to collaborate, share ideas, and help each other out. Remember the water cooler? Many of the more innovative businesses, most famously Google, create places to gather that are free of work intrusions. Some have a "notification-free" zone, where there are no beeps, buzzes, or flashing screens demanding attention, which creates time for quality personal interaction to take place. What works in the workplace is also good personal practice. Give yourself time during the day for just spacing out. Get out for a walk. Putter in your garden. Meditate. Do a Stoic exercise. Have coffee with a workmate. You will be refreshed and eager to go back to work.

Natural rhythms are important to acknowledge and honor in your life as well as in your workday. There is a time and season for everything, as the Bible states so poetically. There is a time to be a full-throated and furious activist and a time to be a mentor to others. A time to be oriented outward, toward the broader world, and a time to focus inward, on yourself and your family. Take pleasure in nature and in the beauty of the world. I find music to be reinvigorating, whether listening to Jorge Ben or the Eroica Trio, or banging away on my guitar. Find your place of peace or passion and visit it regularly.

Burnout isn't just from working too hard. You may find yourself losing your belief in yourself or feel your efforts are wasted or ineffective. Do you have someone you can share your fears and worries with? Don't expect your life partner to be your only confidante. Because they love you, it's hard for them to play the necessary role of critic. Go for a beer with a friend, have tea with a mentor, or find someone who isn't a family member to walk and talk with. Sometimes just talking about your work with someone can give you a clearer picture of what is causing you doubt and weighing you down. Be open to new paths. There are many ways to contribute to a better world. And remember, caring for the world doesn't exclude caring for yourself and the people you love.

CHALLENGE #7

Staying Open to New Ideas

Have you ever been driven crazy by a young child who, having learned the word *why*, can't seem to say anything else? As a young father, I found my match in my sons when they were two. When they asked me, "Why?" I would respond with my best understanding of physical phenomena and social behavior, translated into language as simple as I could muster, only to be asked again, "Why?" Children's innate and insatiable curiosity about the world isn't just about bugging their parents. Seriously. Curiosity is the way we master our world. And the child's brain is growing exponentially at this age, forming new neuronal connections with every new discovery. This is how they gain the knowledge and tools to understand their world and live well in it. My youngest son, Lars, never tired of dismantling the garden wall with his friend, in search of bugs, worms, and spiders. I'd rebuild it only to see it come down again as they continued their investigations. Letting them tear down that wall nurtured their curiosity and taught them about the world and how it works (including about gravity—ouch!).

Curiosity is a powerful tool to engage adults, as well. When we help people explore the effects of change, through imagining different futures, we empower them in ways extending well beyond the issue at hand. Giving them the permission to ask questions, to seek out explanations, to understand how the world works. People want to know why. They don't like to be told "because" any more than children do. Leaders can guide this discovery process by asking a question such as, "What would it look like if we were successful?" Taking people through a process of discovery—rather than handing them a completed product and expecting them to buy into it—engages them on a much deeper level. They can see how their participation and input make a difference. When people know how things tick—how decisions will impact their future as well as how to influence those decisions—they become active; that is, they become true citizens.

As a leader, do you model a willingness to learn and openness to new ideas? One of the people I admired was the chief operating officer of Metro, Michael Jordan. He would often say, "I reserve the right to be smarter today than I was yesterday." I think he said this as much as a reminder to himself as to others that the world is a complicated place. We can't know everything. But if we are open to new information we can change our actions and attitudes to do better every day.

- Do you research issues and ask people involved why they are pursuing a particular direction before taking a position?
- Are you willing to adopt new ideas even if they don't fit with your previous positions?
- Do you make a habit of asking others for their perspectives?
- Do you show interest and delight in the learning process yourself?

Almost every challenge is an opportunity to learn new things and to meet new people. Being open to new ideas and perspectives helped me be more creative in coming up with solutions to difficult or contentious problems. Being open to the opinions and ideas of others also helps build the alliances and relationships necessary to actually get things done. Learning is the deepest expression of what it means to be alive and truly human. Like the two-year-old, if I am learning I feel that I am growing. *I am a stronger leader if I also model for others this willingness and eagerness to learn.* Life is just too short and the world too big to get stuck on any one idea, no matter how good it once seemed to us or how much effort we've sunk into it. The more we can reach out and connect with others, to learn from them what works and what doesn't, the stronger we are as leaders.

The incredible accessibility of information online can make it tempting to focus on Google, Yahoo!, or Bing for our ideas. The Internet is great for getting inspiration and examples as well as for connecting with people who already agree with you. But making change in your community requires that you connect directly with your fellow citizens. Ideas, data, and arguments from elsewhere can help build your case, but surprisingly few decisions are made solely on data or logical arguments. Desires and fears have a huge influence, especially when we think our neighborhoods or lives will be affected. We can only address people's emotional reactions to new ideas by building relationships with the people in our community.

CHALLENGE #8

Embracing Failure

But what if I fail? That big question stares us in the face every time we contemplate starting a new project or getting involved with a new cause. My answer is "So what if you do?" So what if you do take on a tough issue and fail to fix it? The world still revolves around the sun, you will still be living and breathing, and you will be wiser and better equipped for the next time! When Thomas Edison was asked about his years spent trying to perfect the incandescent lightbulb, he replied, "I have not failed. I just found ten thousand ways that did not work."

Read that again: "I have not failed. I just found ten thousand ways that did not work."

What a wonderful world we'd live in if we all thought more like Thomas Edison! In chapter 2 I wrote about the Stoics' approach and the strategies they used to gain perspective on life. Their advice on failure is that worrying that you will fail wastes your time and your potential. If you can respond as Edison did to each of his "ten thousand ways that did not work"—seeing each attempt as an important opportunity to learn—then it won't matter if your project doesn't succeed the first time or ends up looking quite different from what you expected when you started out.

When you stop fearing failure, you can focus on the joy of doing. And that includes the pleasure of meeting and getting to know new people and discovering new perspectives. Sure, celebrate victories. But also celebrate and learn from setbacks.

My love of bugs and creeks led me to study biology in college. Science is basically a willingness to test new ideas and learn from each attempt, *especially* the ones that don't work. Too often people get discouraged if they don't succeed in making change happen the first time. When you measure success by relationships created, strategies tested, and ideas generated through the mix of ideas and perspectives, every effort you make is a step toward success. Even if a particular strategy fails.

Revolutions are rare and their outcomes generally disappointing even to the revolutionaries. Societies usually change slowly as we come up with new approaches to old problems usually through a process of trial and error. Our engagement and passion can spur on and help direct this evolutionary process—which is why being an active citizen is so important. Even unsuccessful attempts to improve the world prepare the way for future change.

Why do we fear failure when I make it sound so fun to try and not succeed? Edison, after all, got rich from his inventions that *did* work. Where is the return for activists who might put years of their lives into their work and still end up getting run over by more powerful interests or continually ignored by society? My optimism comes from looking back over my life and seeing many incredible changes for the better. When I was young, cities were polluted and abandoned to the poor and powerless. Rivers were full of raw sewage. We feared dying from atomic bomb attacks. Riots followed multiple assassinations of revered leaders. Blacks and other minorities faced pervasive discrimination, unnoticed by most white Americans.

Today I see revitalized cities, protected wilderness, clean air and water, safe food, and a black president of the United States. So much has changed *because people refused to accept the status quo*. Ordinary people pushed for changes in laws and behavior to stop pollution, end discrimination, protect wilderness, and more. Because our lives are short, progress always seems slow. I know that there is still much to do. Plus, new challenges arise all the time, like climate change and the increasingly large gap between rich and poor. Taking the long view helps me counsel others, not to be patient—please, be impatient with inequity and injustice and neglect!—but to recognize that as stone is worn away by water, even seemingly immovable prejudice and powerful special interests can be changed by consistent, committed pressure.

Like Thomas Edison, give yourself and others the permission to fail ten thousand times. You will succeed!

CHAPTER 4 BLUEPRINT FOR CHANGE

In this chapter, I gave you a laundry list of challenges you will probably face one day. And hopefully I gave you some good advice for coping with them. Yes, you will face many challenges as you try to effect change in the world, but let me assure you that the victories, the friendships, and the adventures will outweigh the hardships you encounter. However, if there are challenges you feel are not addressed in this book or ones I've addressed that you've found some good ways to surmount, I hope you'll let me know. My email address is in the book's epilogue.

CHAPTER 5

MOVING THROUGH CONFLICT TO GET RESULTS

*"Whenever you're in conflict with someone, there is one
factor that can make the difference between damaging your
relationship and deepening it. That factor is attitude."*
—William James

onflict is something too big to be considered a mere "challenge." It is a condi-
tion, part of the environment of an activist. Your ability to manage conflict—
not avoid or survive conflict—will make a huge difference in whether your efforts
succeed. Whatever you are fighting for, there will usually be an equally passionate
side fighting against. In this chapter we'll explore the best ways to manage conflict
on the way to achieving your goals.

Despite all the stories about how deeply divided we are in American society,
there is a lot of research that casts doubts on how deep these divides really go. Much
social division is hype pushed by those who profit from dividing us, such as Fox
News and the propaganda machines funded by corporate interests. Underneath it

all, there are many fundamental values we share that can be starting points for our conversations about change.

Adam Davis is a respected pollster in Oregon. Over the last thirty years, Adam has asked thousands of Oregonians about the things they care about and find important. His clients include many companies and government agencies. Every ten years or so he does a major statewide poll called the Oregon Values and Belief Survey, exploring the underlying values driving Oregonians' attitudes and behavior. He has observed how Oregonians' values have changed—and stayed the same—for over thirty years. His data challenge the prevailing myth that there is a strong divide in Oregon on key issues, including the environment, the role of government, and the economy. Oregonians of all political persuasions and from all around the state tell him that they strongly value the same basic things about living in Oregon. They value Oregon's natural beauty. They value high environmental quality—clean air and clean water. They value Oregon's strong sense of community! They want an economy that provides a good living for families and protects natural systems. They even find Oregon's cloudy climate one of its major attractions. Even on the politically charged issue of climate change, the survey found in 2013 that 71% of Oregonians see climate change as a problem that we need to do something about. These findings echo similar research from around the country. Despite the hot rhetoric on particular issues, Americans of all stripes highly value health, family, nature, and community.[9]

As leaders we must challenge those who frame disagreements as rooted in fundamental and irreconcilable differences between people. This isn't easy. Putting people into boxes is so pervasive. The media is especially guilty of this, giving everybody and every idea a label—progressive, conservative, red, blue, right, left. But remember Adam's survey: we are more alike—we all care deeply about the same things—than we are different. Let's focus debate on the best ways to protect the things we care

---

9.   In EcoAmerica's 2006 American Environmental Values Survey on American attitudes about the environment, 93% of respondents said they love to be outdoors, 92% think that children should spend more time outdoors, and 85% think that every town should have land with nature trails nearby. 83% believe that we can achieve environmental protection and economic growth at the same time.

about and respond to threats to them. By acknowledging how much we value the same things, it is possible to build workable strategies that will be widely accepted.

In 2014 there were surprising alliances between groups usually seen as bitter opponents. The Tea Party and the NAACP have teamed up in Missouri to pass bills to limit the practice of local governments funding significant portions of their budgets through traffic fines and penalties, even imprisoning people for failing to pay and then charging them to get out of jail! Since this happens mostly to low-income, minority people, the NAACP has a natural interest. The Tea Party has concerns about growing government spending as well as what it sees as government's intrusion into people's lives. On the national level, the liberal group MoveOn.org is collaborating with conservative FreedomWorks to reform criminal justice policy. "You can't keep fighting the caricature of the other side if you've sat down with them and had a cup of coffee," said the head of FreedomWorks, Matt Kibbe.[10]

When I was on the Metro Council, we hired Adam to conduct focus groups, asking people what they thought about growth, transportation, and land use. He also asked about climate change and energy use. I watched the recording from one session in which a man stated repeatedly and strongly his opposition to government edicts on reducing energy use or making driving more difficult and expensive. He said he didn't believe that climate change was actually happening. Then something prompted him to talk about energy conservation, a topic it turned out he was very interested in. He spoke of how he had borrowed a device that measured energy consumption from his neighborhood association office. Using this, he found that many of his appliances and electronic devices continued to use electricity when not in use. Oh, did that make him mad! He called them energy vampires and urged everyone in the group to get one of these devices themselves and to unplug their electrical devices when not being used. Waste was something this person just could not abide. "Saving energy" and "reducing electricity bills" were completely acceptable ways for him to act on the environmental values he shared with others in the group, even as he resisted government action and denied climate change. His abhorrence of

---

10. "Law Enforcement Concerns Create Unlikely Alliances in Missouri and Beyond," *New York Times*, February 15, 2015

waste in all its forms—a value shared by Green Party members and conservatives alike—opened up a new way to talk about land use and transportation using ideas like efficiency and choice that transcended left-right framing.

A strong leader can help disputing parties uncover the underlying, often unspoken values they share. By starting where we agree—we all want our families to be healthy and safe, for example—you frame problems your community faces in a way that most everyone will find compelling. Using a common language of deeply held values, you can keep moving forward even when there are disagreements over strategy and tactics.

- Remind people of what they share.
- Ask them to envision a future that honors these values.
- Challenge them to find ways to achieve that get us to that future.
- Hold them—and yourself—accountable to do what it takes to get there.

FINDING OUT WHAT YOUR COMMUNITY VALUES

A Key to Successful Leadership

As a way to institutionalize our strategy of approaching decisions in this way, my six fellow members of the Metro Council and I adopted the following language to guide our agency's work:

> *Values trump data when it comes to decision making. People make decisions consciously and unconsciously based on their values, and then utilize data to rationalize and support their choice. For individuals to maintain a lasting commitment to an issue as a personal priority, and to hold a conviction that leads to action, the issue must connect to closely held personal values.*
>
> *—Building Public Will*

We often talk about *what* we want, or *how* we think something should be done, but the reasons *why* usually remain unspoken. Every decision we make reflects values we believe to be important, although we rarely speak about these values. When asked *why* we think such and such should happen, we usually respond with something like, "it's just the right thing to do" or "it's only fair." Underlying these vague sentiments are assumptions about what we think is important. Uncovering these assumptions is a valuable part of any problem-solving process. Getting people to articulate what they value will create opportunities for finding solutions that can overcome ideological or partisan divides.

Talking about values can be tricky—after all, people want action, not talk. Ask for their patience. Take time to talk about what is important in their lives. Have them tell you and others why. Try exercises such as having them talk with another person about how the issue affected their lives or even have them write for a couple of minutes about their experiences. Help them see connections with others in the group. By refraining from jumping right into debating strategy and talking points, understanding and perspectives will have time to develop. The goal is to ensure everyone's contribution will be meaningful and lasting.

FROM THE TRENCHES

Fighting for a Long-Lived Tradition

Outdoor School is an Oregon tradition. Sixth-grade students have been going to a weeklong outdoor school for sixty years. It's a great thing. But like many great things in public education—arts, physical education, and music—Outdoor School is disappearing from Oregon schools. I helped my son's sixth-grade class raise money to save Outdoor School in Portland Public Schools in 2003. Later, as a Metro councilor, I successfully convinced my fellow councilors to invest over one million dollars annually to support Outdoor School in the Portland metropolitan region. This was still not enough.

I asked for help.

And here's what my wise friends told me: "No."

They said they wouldn't help me if my goal was only to raise enough money for Outdoor School in the metropolitan region. They reminded me that Outdoor School was an Oregon tradition, part of a shared heritage linking rural and urban residents. And it was disappearing throughout Oregon, not just in the Portland area. Rural and poor districts were especially affected. They reminded me that Outdoor School's purpose is to create scientifically and environmentally literate citizens who value Oregon's incredible heritage of nature and abundant natural resources. And all Oregon kids needed this.

As I write this book, I am launching a new statewide coalition to make this happen. It is a coalition that includes timber companies as well as environmental groups. Educators and high-tech entrepreneurs. Farmers and scientists. They are coming together because they share a love and concern for the future of Oregon that transcends political divisions. We share the knowledge that the only way we can solve the big challenges facing us is by ensuring that our citizens have the tools and understanding to make wise decisions in how they live, how they vote, and how they act. And that getting kids—all kids—out into nature, learning science by digging in the mud and tromping the woods, and sharing meals with strangers who become friends, is how we build good citizens. This diverse coalition has a good chance of winning dedicated funding for this venerable tradition. (Our latest polling shows more than 65% of Oregon voters support raising taxes to send all kids to a full Outdoor School program.)

DEFINING OUTCOMES: GOING FROM VALUES TO ACTION

If defining values is about understanding what motivates us to get up in the morning and do what we do, defining outcomes is about how we take those values and express them in the world. Most people would say that caring for their families is a very important value. But how do we do that? There are a variety of conditions that are necessary for family well-being. We all need decent housing. We all need medical care when we are ill. We all need nourishing food. We all need protection from harm. How can families get these? A strong economy with jobs accessible to everyone will help with housing and food. Likewise, an accessible and affordable health care system is needed. Streets with sidewalks and safe crossings will protect us when we travel. A responsive police force along with social expectations of lawful behavior will keep us secure.

Ongoing debates about the Affordable Care Act (ACA) show how even when values are deeply shared—such as the importance of a healthy family—there is no guarantee there will be agreement on the best way to get there. Is it best to deliver health care through a private insurer or a government agency? Is health care really the issue at all? Since a huge percentage of health problems are caused by poor diet, shouldn't we be banning fatty, sugary foods? Or is this the responsibility of the family?

Even though we share basic values and desired outcomes (a healthy family, for instance, and access to health care), we will still debate strategies to achieve those outcomes and further those values. It may never have been possible for Congress to step away from its interest group– and corporate backer–defined limits to come up with a bipartisan health-care bill. But maybe if Congress had started by talking about the best ways to ensure Americans are healthy, we could have seen a radically different approach to health that addressed transportation policy, farm subsidies, chemical regulation, tobacco and alcohol control, and other components of what makes us healthy.

TRY IT NOW #13

Creating Goals That Inspire, Focus, and Motivate Action

Putting all this down on paper can help clarify and focus your efforts. Thoughtful preparation—where you are going as well as how and why you are heading there—is critical to effectively communicating your intent and rallying others to your cause. How can you know whether the goals you set meet these standards? Try running them through the following set of questions:

Goal: To achieve X change by X date (this could be organizational goals or policy goals such as "grow membership to two thousand members by January 2016" or "adopt carbon tax in Oregon of fifteen dollars per ton by 2017" or "plant twenty thousand trees in the city of Portland in five years."

SPECIFIC	Is your goal or outcome well defined and clear?
MEASURABLE	Do you have a way to measure whether you are reaching your goal? What criteria are you using to measure success?
ACHIEVABLE, BUT NOT SIMPLE	Does the goal stretch you, while being reasonable, given your resources and influence?
MOTIVATIONAL	Does the goal inspire you and others?
RELEVANT	Is the goal relevant to your vision, mission, and responsibilities?
TIME-FRAMED	Can you achieve your goal within the timeline you've set?

Now try it with your goals:

Goal: _____

SPECIFIC	
MEASURABLE	
ACHIEVABLE, BUT NOT SIMPLE	
MOTIVATIONAL	
RELEVANT	
TIME-FRAMED	

KNOWING HOW TO ASK, NOT JUST WHAT TO ASK FOR

Probably every sassy child from every region of the United States has heard the folk adage "You will catch more flies with honey than vinegar." Certainly I have, because my mother said it often enough to me! I recalled her words just the other day when I was at a Portland Planning and Sustainability Commission hearing on the hot topic of parking in neighborhoods. The room was full of people angry about city policies that allowed new apartments to be built without parking spaces. City policy allowed new residential buildings along streets with good bus service to have little or no off-street parking to encourage lower building costs and rents.

I saw Terry Parker there. Terry is a Portland activist I'd heard from often over the years. He loves to rail against "freeloading bicyclists." We chatted about why we were at yet another public meeting together. Had I seen that he'd recently been quoted in the newspaper on another issue, he asked? "I really zinged them and it got printed!" he proudly declared. "Wait until you hear what I'm going to say today." Knowing Terry and his love of the precisely timed rant in front of public bodies, I asked him if his previous testimony had any impact on the decisions made that day. He said, no, whatever group he had addressed hadn't done as he had recommended—but he had been *published!* We then talked a bit about effectiveness and activism. I've heard lots of impassioned people using plenty of strong language in their efforts to influence others. Yet I've found that harsh language and personal attacks typically only harden positions rather than change minds. No one likes to feel bullied or attacked.

DRIZZLING ON THE HONEY

Societies develop rules of etiquette to ease interactions between citizens, interest groups, businesses, and government. Driving on the right, waiting in line for your turn, allowing others to speak—these are all social conventions we agree to in order for society to function smoothly. For example, most government bodies use Robert's Rules of Order to manage discussion and debate. Such rules of engagement are based on the idea that all viewpoints should be able to be heard while ensuring an orderliness to the process so that decisions will move forward. You may use a simplified version yourself without even knowing it, such as when you ask a group to make sure everyone has a chance to speak or when you tell your kids not to take seconds until everyone has been served.

We use rules or social conventions to create predictable and transparent processes for negotiating between the various interests and ideas people have. Similarly, a good government process is one where everyone understands the rules and knows that their concerns will be heard. Rules can become very complex—one reason we have so many lawyers—with prescribed timelines and formats for comments, for example. Learning how to play the game is an important skill for activists and leaders. Because once the bulldozers arrive, it is usually too late to make a difference.

In complex, bureaucratic societies like ours, transparency and clarity can be elusive things. We have so many levels of government—each with its own set of rules, responsibilities, and acronyms—that it can seem impossible to understand, much less effectively try to influence, their decisions. Hence, the huge industry of lobbying. We hire the expertise needed to work the system because we have made the system too complex for amateurs—us citizens. *The secret to effective lobbying for citizen activists is knowing that within the maze of rules and process requirements there are people.* People make things happen. People with responsibilities and commitments to their work, yes, but also people with families, interests, and feelings. *Too often activists forget that people are making the decisions.* Which is where being polite and friendly comes in.

Being polite and friendly doesn't mean you can't be determined and unrelenting in pursuit of your agenda. The effective use of social norms can advance your cause. The power in being polite is that it can bond you with the people behind the system. Being polite as a strategy to effect change is what I call the "honey factor." When you enter into a relationship with people on human terms, they are more likely to help. Some will even go so far as to act as your inside informants, letting you know when critical decisions are going to be made or sharing key pieces of difficult-to-find information. They can help you be more successful by guiding you through the system because of your personal connection.

FROM THE TRENCHES

Persistence and Politeness

Here's a real-world example. It can be hard to believe in a time when cities are falling over themselves to be "bicycle friendly," but not that long ago people who rode bicycles were seen as hobbyists, a special interest group, or even nuisances without a legitimate place in the transportation system. Now, New York City competes with San Francisco, Chicago, and Los Angeles to build bicycle paths, run bike-lending programs, and promote cycling as a healthy, affordable alternative to car-choked streets. Portland was at the forefront of this change in attitude, but it didn't happen easily or overnight. It wasn't made easier by the fact that people who rode bikes weren't in any way united as a community, even if noncyclists, including government officials, lumped us all together. There were the recreational riders, some of whom fit the stereotype of Lycra-clad athletes who just wanted to ride, and ride fast. There were the urban planner and environmentalist policy wonks, who rode bicycles as practical transportation and saw the bicycle as a tool of urban transformation. Then there were those who saw bicycling as a way to protest against a consumerist, environmentally destructive society—they came together under the banner of Critical Mass, an event more than an organization.

Trying to organize such a diverse group of people simply because they all rode bicycles wasn't easy. Although they all wanted to be safe when riding, the cyclists belonged to every point on the political spectrum: libertarian, anarchist, and everything in between. Some of the recreational riders actually opposed the idea of advocacy because they thought asking the government to do something for cycling was inappropriate (*they* didn't see a problem, only a fun challenge in racing traffic). Many Critical Mass participants embraced confrontation as the only meaningful strategy, reasoning that the state was rotten and engaging with its agents, whether politicians, planners, or police, was only accepting an evil system. This put us middle-of-the-roaders (so to speak!) alone with our approach of active engagement with government. While we did employ classic community-organizing strategies such as recruiting and activating volunteers to lobby, we also made a point of developing professional and personal relationships with the various agencies that had a role to play in transportation. This included the police, state and local transportation agencies, school districts, zoning and parking departments, et cetera. By being respectful, doing our homework (understanding how and when decisions were made, who was responsible for them, and how best to offer ideas and comments), and, especially, never attacking staff or politicians personally, we earned our way to being key participants in many decisions. In a short decade, we ignited and achieved a major transformation of the City of Portland as well as the metro area and state.

A DASH OF VINEGAR: CAN WE BE TOO NICE?

Is there a danger in being too nice? As Frederick Douglass said, power will rarely give up power unless it is forced to. Is there a good time to let our anger or frustration show?

Standards of what is proper behavior *are* created by the powerful. Etiquette, including rules and procedures, can be used to control demands from society. It can also be used to limit debate by controlling who can speak, when they can speak and for how long, and what they can talk about and in what format. The widely used Robert's Rules of Order, created to manage debate among equals, can make it difficult for alternative perspectives to be heard. Is it ever desirable, advantageous, or necessary to be "impolite," to not follow the established rules of engagement? It is a valid, strategic question to ask.

FROM THE TRENCHES

Getting Played by Playing Too Nice

Early in my career as an activist, I volunteered for a city committee charged with updating the zoning code to include bicycle parking as part of new buildings. As a newbie, I felt like it was a victory to even be at the table, where the action was. A player, at last! It was only later that I realized that my being inexperienced as well as flattered allowed others to use their superior knowledge of how to play the game to outmaneuver me. I ended up hurting my cause (improving conditions for bicycle use) and wasting lots of my time. I eventually realized that the others at the table weren't interested in coming up with workable solutions. They opposed any new requirements and used their knowledge of the system—the rules of etiquette—to delay the process and weaken the final recommendation.

- **The downtown building owners' representative** had no interest in doing anything that would increase costs or change how his clients did business, regardless of studies showing how accommodating cyclists would benefit them. He was paid by the hour for attending the meetings, so a quick solution clearly wasn't his goal!
- Another member, representing **the local school district**, feared increased liability for the district if students were encouraged to ride bikes to school. Also being paid to attend, he was content to have endless discussions and drafts upon drafts prepared.
- The **city staffer** could see that any solution he put forward would displease one constituency or the other and didn't have much incentive to push for closure. The bicycle community, being the weakest participant at that time, was the easiest to ignore.

Originally, there were many other citizen members on the committee, including architects, small business representatives, and planners. The endless and circular nature of the discussions drove them away. I remained, naive and polite, sticking it out through three years of delay and obstructionism from those who, I finally realized, had no interest in seeing any new policies adopted. In the end, both big building developers and school districts were exempted from providing bicycle parking! I walked away defeated. I didn't realize for a long time that being too polite contributed to my failure.

MIXING HONEY WITH THE VINEGAR

When honey doesn't work, what are your alternatives? Begin by understanding your interests first of all, then the interests of the other party. Knowing what you want is easy; knowing what others want can be difficult. Discussions are usually focused on what people say they want (their issues), not what they really care about (their interests). In the FROM THE TRENCHES example above, our committee discussed things like numbers of bicycle racks per square foot of buildings and other technical details, not why it might be in the interest of building owners and school districts to promote bicycling to their facilities. They saw any new requirements as just costing them money. Bringing these interests into the open may have brought out different strategies that addressed their needs while resulting in better bike parking.

What other things could I have done differently? Insisted on clear deadlines and expectations for the committee's work. Every time you get asked to represent your interest, ask first: What is the charge of this group? When is the work supposed to be done (only the most difficult issues should take more than six months to a year)? Who is in charge—that is, who is the elected official or upper-level staff who is ultimately responsible? Refuse to waste your time huffing and puffing with people who can't actually make a decision. Reserve the right to walk away if the process doesn't meet *your* goals. Don't worry about theirs. Continue to pressure city leaders through grassroots activism—letters and postcards to elected officials and the media, demonstrations targeting recalcitrant players, et cetera. Finally, recognize that the other party's interests may be better served by not coming to a timely conclusion. (See Know Your BATNA further along.)

Of course, the real world isn't as simple as choosing one tactic to the exclusion of the other. *Rules need to be broken when critically important perspectives are not allowed to be heard or the process is being used to prevent change from happening.* Here are some ways to reduce the likelihood of special interests manipulating the process:

- Get agreement up front about timelines, expected outcomes, and who should be at the table for any decision.

- Decide ahead of time how much time and what kind of resources you and your organization are willing to commit to the inside game. Have an outside game in mind (a plan B).

- Insist on inviting other voices to the table. Insist on having meetings where and when the affected community can participate. This is inconvenient to agency staff and paid lobbyists who prefer to work nine to five. They will resist. Challenge them to offer another way to engage the affected community and insist that this be part of the decision-making process.

- If the others resist any of this, go to the top, to the elected decision maker, and ask them to set clear goals and timelines. After all, you're a citizen, and these guys and gals work for you!

- If they don't listen, share your story with the media, being clear that this isn't about process alone; it's about good governance and a more inclusive vision of community.

- Organize! Get others to call or write. Because so many people never take the time to contact their elected officials, hearing from just a small number of constituents will often get results when you are feeling stymied.

- Keep your independence! Remember that you always have the option of appealing to the community directly. It is so easy to get lost in the gray muddle of midlevel bureaucracy.

- Finally, reserve the right to walk away.

Do this with grace and love, but don't be afraid to put on a little heat. Avoid being sour or bitter. After all, these people are your neighbors. Vindictiveness and personal attacks rarely work. People may be flat-out wrong or bullheaded or self-interested in ways that you think are bad for your community, but you will probably work with them again someday in the future. If you use your strengths—persuasion, telling a better story, rallying the community around a better idea—you can achieve your goal while maintaining a reputation as an honest problem solver, which will enable you to work with others, even those who might have opposed you at one time.

SOMETIMES EVEN HONEY WON'T SOOTHE EVERYTHING

"Honey" helps to avoid conflict. "Vinegar" may be needed to make sure you are heard. So, as I said at the outset of this chapter, it should be obvious by now that conflict will be a part of your life as an activist. Of course, conflict is part of *all* life, right? One of the first lessons our parents taught us when we were young was how to share. Childhood's a conflict-ridden environment if there ever was one! *Someone took my cookie! Give it back!* Therefore, learning how to deal with conflict in constructive and loving ways is critical.

Now when I find myself in disagreement with someone, my personal challenge is pausing long enough so I respond strategically rather than emotionally. I'm still worried about losing that cookie! Our genes program us to either fight or run away from conflict: the adrenaline starts flowing way before our conscious mind can analyze the situation. It can be very difficult to maintain the detachment needed to analyze the situation and respond in ways that move our agendas forward.

Being rational in the heat of the moment is hard. Practicing ways to manage conflict ahead of time can help you avoid responding emotionally or making a decision you may regret. If you've ever watched a courtroom drama, you know lawyers deliberately use people's emotions to get them to do things—like confess to murder on the witness stand! Some people will deliberately exploit our tendency to respond emotionally to conflict to get us to agree to something we would never do unless we were upset, scared, or angry. You can get into similar difficulty if you feel your interests are threatened or your voice is being ignored. You may make a concession or refuse to hear an innovative solution because you are responding emotionally, not strategically.

This is when you should take a break. It's okay to step back from the difficult situation if you are feeling pressured. Remember the old ad slogan for a famous soda? The pause that refreshes? Don't make decisions or commit to anything in the heat of the moment. Step away. Go to your allies to get another perspective.

Reflect on this question: Is the conflict a personal one—are you feeling insulted or attacked?—or is the conflict between your values and goals and those of the person or group you are struggling with? Unless you address why you are in conflict, you will just face the same situation again. Even if you go out and get reinforcements—polishing your arguments with shiny new data or adding members to your coalition—you can bet your antagonist is out doing the exact same thing. It's our societal pattern of conflict resolution: build a bigger army than your opponent so you can crush them. But there are other strategies, ones that use conflict as a way to come to better solutions.

DON'T AVOID CONFLICT, USE IT

Conflict tells us a lot about the people we work with, helping us to understand their strengths as well as their weaknesses. Conflict can also bring new ideas and information to the surface. Because we associate conflict with anger and personal animosity (negative emotions that make people uncomfortable), most groups try to suppress conflict by adopting norms of behavior, consciously or not, that discourage the expression of alternative views and ideas. Put this way, who wouldn't agree that suppressing open debate is a bad thing? But get in the middle of a fray in a room full of glowering looks and sharp words, and the natural impulse is to avoid conflict, not welcome it.

But we need people to share their ideas and perspectives so our understanding of issues, group dynamics, and options is as rich as possible. Smoothing over conflicts will leave some ideas and perspectives off the table, ideas that might be critical pieces of a successful solution. It is important to manage conflict to protect our common humanity because big arguments leave people feeling hurt, ineffective, and exhausted, and they aren't helpful. Most conflicts, though, don't get so dramatic, but unless acknowledged, conflict drains the energy and enthusiasm right out of a group. A sign of an unhealthy conflict is when a group keeps circling back on issues and can't seem to make decisions and people keep raising questions you thought had been resolved. This quiet *withholding of consent* can be just as debilitating as out-and-out fighting.

We need to acknowledge that every time we get a group of people together, there will be differences of opinion, different levels of knowledge about an issue, different perspectives based on personal and professional backgrounds, and different levels of commitment. This is why we work in groups! To benefit from the richness and variety of our experience. By acknowledging and valuing difference, we can elicit these ideas and perspectives in an organized and fruitful way.

SOME STRATEGIES FOR USING CONFLICT

As a leader, it's your job to give your staff and supporters productive ways to contribute, ways that honor their desire to contribute and be part of a force for good. Conflict often arises when people don't feel that they've had a chance to be heard, when they feel their contributions aren't valued, and when they feel patronized. There are four strategies I've used to harness people's energy and passion in ways that validate their engagement and contribution. Remember, honoring others' ideas doesn't mean abandoning your vision—it's about taking those ideas and incorporating them into that vision. These strategies can also help people learn about what works and what is doable, expanding their capabilities while forging cohesion in the group.

The four strategies:

- Listen to understand.
- Role reversal.
- SWOT analysis.
- Brainstorm.

Listen to Understand: Also called active listening, this technique works well in one-on-one situations but can be adapted into a group exercise. Divide people up into groups of two and afterward have people share what they learned. Designate one person to be the listener. Their task is just to listen while the other person talks, without commenting. The listener then repeats what they heard back to the speaker, in a shortened, paraphrased form, such as "What I think I heard you say is . . ." The key here is the speaker determines whether their meaning was accurately captured. This can be much more challenging than it sounds! Especially when dealing with hot topics. Once the speaker agrees that the listener has gotten it right, have them switch roles. This may not be necessary as you might have an Aha! moment where you both really understand the basis for the current differences in perception or maybe the way to fix a behavior that is upsetting.

Role Reversal: This one can be really fun in a group, especially if the group is made up of people with a mix of interests and perspectives. This exercise takes some preparation and buy-in from everyone involved in the process. It is most useful as part of a larger problem-solving effort. Organize into groups of six to ten people. Make sure to mix it up—don't let people sit with their colleagues. Assign roles to each person in the group representing the varied interests in the room.

A sample might be: businessperson, environmental activist, worried PTA member, libertarian, et cetera. Write down each role on a slip of paper and have each person take one. Give the group a problem related to the issue at hand but not necessarily the exact issue. Ask people to make an argument from the perspective of the role they've been assigned, rather than from their own perspective. People usually will really get into this, sometimes exaggerating the position of the role, delineating the issues at hand more clearly (freed from the bounds of politeness—they're only "pretending," after all). But serious work gets done because in order to play the role well, people have to try to understand another person's perspective.

SWOT Analysis: **S**trength, **W**eakness, **O**pportunity, and **T**hreat analysis is a good method for examining the internal state of an organization, as well as a way to understand the world in which it operates. Take two sheets of flip chart paper and draw a line down the middle of each one. On one side of the first sheet, list your group's strengths (what you do well) and on the other your group's weaknesses (what you do poorly). When done with those, turn to the second sheet. Of one side of the second sheet, make a list of opportunities coming up (what you can take advantage of to advance your mission) and on the other the threats you face (what may make it difficult or damage your chances of success). Just let people shout out ideas for each list. Don't worry about refining these ideas at first (see the next section on brainstorming). When the group has run out of steam, go back over what you wrote down and look for patterns in each category. Are there ideas that came up in different ways? Those will probably be the key issues to explore more. Ask the group to identify and prioritize the most pressing issues or exciting ideas. I find that consensus comes pretty easily because people are usually thinking about these questions already and the SWOT exercise brings their ideas and concerns to the surface.

Brainstorm: If you get stuck, brainstorm! I really like brainstorming and try to get people to make it a habit to use it in many situations when problem solving is called for. Most people enjoy the opportunity to share their ideas without fear of being judged or having to defend them. The goal is to explore what's out there, not to make a decision, yet.

Here's how it works:

1. Set up ground rules for the brainstorm.
    a. Every idea is a good idea. Debating for merit is for later.
    b. Ask questions for understanding and clarification.
    c. Encourage building on ideas. ("Yes, and . . .")
    d. One person speaks at a time.
    e. Everyone participates.
2. Put all the ideas up on a board or flip chart so everybody's ideas get equal billing.
3. After everyone has had the chance to chime in, with the group's help, lump similar ideas together. Get permission to lump or create categories. Engage people in the process.
4. List idea summaries. Now is the time to discuss the merits of each idea. Which ones have promise for advancing your interests? Are there ways that different approaches can be combined so you can be more effective at your work? You can do a pros-and-cons chart or anything that feels comfortable as a way to capture the conversation.

You can also do quickie brainstorms whenever you want to get a lot of information and participation out of people. Just use the same process. No need to get all formal with it. Encourage brainstorming as a part of everyday problem solving. Creativity and teamwork will increase as your group gets more familiar and excited about how brainstorming opens up possibilities and overcomes differences.

DISRUPTING NEGATIVE BEHAVIOR

When things get tense and you see that your team is losing hope for progress, propose something off the wall to get people out of their defensive, angry state. Help them get into a place where they feel safe to exercise their imagination and passion. Simply directing everyone's attention to the front of the room and engaging them in problem solving can disrupt confrontational patterns. Use any of the techniques above. Some other conflict-disrupting techniques include rearranging the chairs in a semicircle rather than rows, getting rid of the table, even getting rid of the chairs and having people stand up or go outside for a walking meeting. You can also break confrontational cycles by asking people to use other ways of communicating. Have them write out their answers to questions on sticky paper and post them on a board before discussing them. Have members of the group read each question aloud and organize them by theme or idea. Can they act out their proposed solution? Can they draw a picture of their imagined future or idea? Create "email-free zones" to encourage people to physically communicate with each other rather than sending yet another email. Leadership is a chance to learn and try new things. Take the opportunity to be creative!

KNOW YOUR BATNA

(Best Alternative to Negotiated Agreement)

To succeed in making change happen you have to be able to negotiate conflict between people, with all their varied interests. Formal and informal negotiation is the most common means of doing this in our society. You will negotiate with the members of your community. You will negotiate with those in power. If the issue is complicated (what isn't!) and involves many interests (what doesn't!) you will be negotiating with everybody! Strong leaders need strong negotiating skills.

Even if you are a good negotiator, you may get to the point in a negotiation where you feel that what is being proposed is just unacceptable to you or your community. Yet if you've invested much in a process, it can be really difficult to quit. In *Getting to Yes*, Roger Fisher and William Ury give great advice about *how not to lose even when you can't or don't win.* Their advice? Decide ahead of time what is most important to you and your community. What is it, that if you agree to any less, means compromising your values or your interests? They call this process defining a BATNA, your Best Alternative to Negotiated Agreement. Coming up with a BATNA isn't always simple. Indeed, just going through the process may make you feel like you are deciding to settle for less even before negotiations begin. Think of it like buying a car. We usually know how much we'd *like* to spend, how much we *can afford* to spend, and how much we *won't* spend *before* we walk into the salesperson's office. If the salesperson can't or won't sell the car to us at a price somewhere within that range, we go to another dealer. Of course, articulating what a community considers their best deal is more complex than buying a car! But the principles are the same.

Do your homework before you start. Check in with your allies and partners. Decide what you want to get out of a negotiation and in what time frame. Refer to this regularly to measure whether the negotiation is helping you achieve your goal. Maybe you'd make more progress pursuing other strategies. There are times when walking away without a deal is better for you than taking what is being offered. At that point, choosing to walk away isn't a loss, even if you leave empty-handed. Negotiation just may not be the way to get what you want. Your counterparts on the other side of the negotiation may need to be pushed harder outside the negotiating setting to get them to improve their offer.

The keys to successful negotiations:

- Know what you want to achieve ahead of time. Consult with your allies regularly outside of negotiating meetings.
- Define your desired outcomes in terms of interests (e.g., better housing options for low-income people) rather than mechanisms (e.g., more money for rent subsidies).
- Be willing to compromise and hear new ideas. Someone might have a better way to achieve your goals that you haven't thought of yet.
- Measure other proposals against your goals and focus on how these proposals do or don't meet those goals rather than on whether they were your idea or not.

- Set a timeline for action, based on your needs, to be able to gauge whether you are making progress or being strung along.
- Be clear to all participants as well as your supporters that you reserve the right to walk away if your interests are being compromised.
- Always, always, be ready with another strategy to pursue your goals.

DON'T LET YOUR PRIDE GET IN THE WAY OF YOUR STRATEGY

It can be embarrassing to return to your community or organization empty-handed. The pressure to deliver for your supporters makes it hard to walk away even after it becomes clear that you aren't achieving your objectives. Again, knowing what you want is key. The more you do ahead of time to define what you want, the stronger your resolve will be and the better you will understand what price—in time, resources, credibility—you are willing to pay in order to reach a resolution. Here are some techniques to avoid agreeing to a bad deal under pressure:

- Call a break so that you can check in with your community. If this is something you are doing on your own, call some trusted friends and just talk it out.
- Remind the others at the table that you are there representing a community's interests, not your own.
- Be clear on the outcomes you are seeking.
- Set as a precondition that any solution agreed to must address these outcomes sufficiently. It takes things out of the realm of the personal.

BEWARE OF PRESSURE TO BE "ONE OF THE GUYS"

In any negotiation, most people want an agreement that meets their needs—on the particular issues, the timing of the process, and the implementation of the results. Often there is an assumed consensus going into the process, founded on the dominant culture's interests and preconceptions. Expect to be pressured to accept this and to go along with the group. If you are a member of the dominant community pushing for it to change, its representatives will appeal to your shared culture as a way to get you to follow its norms, to be "one of the guys." Your efforts to change the process—getting new voices to the table or advocating nonmainstream ideas—may be called "impolite."

Recall that etiquette is a formalization of current or past power relations. Nondominant communities and individuals may be ignored or patronized under the guise of enforcing norms of behavior. Even when their issues *are* recognized as valid, they are often told to be "reasonable" (that is, to conform to the dominant culture's ideas of a solution) and lower their expectations. Putting the responsibility for avoiding conflict on disempowered communities and interests is a way for those in power to avoid acknowledging inequity and to downplay demands for new priorities. Recognize that conflict is natural when there is inequity and this conflict makes people uncomfortable. Don't let admonitions to "get along" and "be part of the solution" deter you from firmly pushing your agenda. Being a successful negotiator means learning to live with this discomfort as well as supporting others to ensure inclusive and honest processes despite this discomfort.

SOMETIMES YOU LOSE

What if you run through plan B and even plan C and nothing works? Sometimes you just lose. Because losing can feel like failing, we often respond to a loss not as a strategic setback but as a personal failure. *Our fear of being seen as a failure* can damage our effectiveness even more than losing a particular point does. There are two dangers to refusing to accept defeat: If we continue to push a failed strategy, we risk burning people out, damaging our credibility as leaders, and wasting time and money; retreat can also give us time to regroup and rethink strategies. At other times, when further compromise only puts our goals further out of reach, ending a struggle is the only way we can keep our integrity.

Sometimes we just have to walk away. But we don't want to give up if there is still a chance of winning. We know it's not true that "you can't fight city hall" because many of us have done it before successfully. You certainly shouldn't give up when there is still a chance of making a difference. But you must be careful to separate your tactical approach from your personal feelings about your abilities or concerns about your reputation.

So, how do you tell the difference between a temporary setback in a process and the time to admit defeat? In the same way leaders prepare themselves for action: checking in with supporters and others in your community, reexamining your goals to see if they are still valid, stepping back and taking a broader look at your organization and community through techniques such as SWOT analysis, and, of course, engaging in self-reflection. Here are some questions to ask:

- Does the problem still exist?
- Have things changed in the world such that your understanding of the problem and your solutions are still valid?
- Finally, have you changed? Are you still the right person to take on this challenge?

There are lots of reasons a particular campaign may not succeed. You may just need more time to build support, create a stronger organization, and make your case more effectively. You may find that what you need is a bigger army—more supporters—before making your move again. Or that an electoral strategy—getting your friends elected—is the only way to change priorities. Maybe it's changing how you talk about your issue, and what you need to do is find help in framing your message—even a name change may be in order—so that people can more easily understand what it is you are trying to accomplish.

If the cause is something you believe in, and others still believe in you (check in with your community!), temporary setbacks are just that: temporary. One of the greatest responsibilities you have as a leader is to be honest with yourself and with your supporters. So take the time for personal and organizational soul-searching.

Go over the above questions and answer them honestly. If the need is still there, if the fire is still there, you haven't been defeated, only tested and made wiser through experience.

BUT WHAT IF YOU WIN? THE CHALLENGES OF SUCCESS

I fervently hope that you will succeed at whatever cause you take on. That you will use the examples and ideas in this book to become a star and help others accomplish great things, too. Are you ready for success?

Leading a successful, growing movement or organization is another challenge that you must prepare for in order to do it well. What began as a brainstorm around a kitchen table with three friends now has a budget, staff, and a community that expects you to deliver. We can get so caught up in the action that we forget to practice thoughtful leadership or think we just don't have time. What are some of the pitfalls of success? How do you prepare for them? Some of these issues have been discussed in other sections of this book, but I want to put a list together here for you to think about as your career and your efforts march on.

- **Founder's syndrome:** Sounds like a disease and it is! Founder's syndrome refers to the struggles a group goes through when the founder fails to grow with the organization. Starting something new from scratch requires entrepreneurial skills including risk taking, extra confidence in one's abilities, and fierce focus. These same traits can be disruptive or at least unproductive in a larger, more mature organization, where cooperation, planning, and consideration of multiple goals are required. Founders have two choices: grow with the organization (which requires adapting one's work style to the group as well as learning new skills), or leave the group (often going on to start another). Those who hang on, while not changing, can throw the group into chaos, alienating supporters, colleagues, and funders.

Advice: Check in regularly with key supporters to help you understand your strengths and weaknesses and how they fit with your group's current needs.

- **Failure to plan for succession:** The world is always changing, and this includes leaders. When I was a director of a nonprofit, as well as when I was in my last term in office, I kept a lookout for the person who could take my place. I mentored people with promise among my volunteers, staff, and board. I recruited capable people to get involved with my group. I would tell my board they had to prepare for finding my replacement, even if I had no immediate plans to leave. This prepares an organization for surprise departures as well as strengthening the group through acquiring skills and recruiting new talent to reduce dependence on one person.

  Advice: Identify, recruit, and train promising leaders.

- **Chasing the dollars:** The pressure of meeting payroll and keeping a large organization going can shift our focus from the goals we want to achieve to how to get enough money to meet organizational demands. The temptation is to chase grants, sometimes taking on projects that aren't exactly what we want to do (but what the funders will fund), hoping the extra cash coming in will somehow support our core work.

  Advice: Keep focus on core mission.

- **Going it alone:** The organization falters when the leader doesn't have the time, focus, or energy to lead. As our groups or movements get bigger and busier, leaders can get isolated, focused on management, donor relations, and personnel issues. This is when delegation is critical.

  Advice: Hire to complement the strengths of staff—for example, hire development and business management help for the leader who is best at policy and inspiration.

- **Forgetting your roots:** Busyness can lead to loss of connection to the community. Our work demands give us less time to talk with those affected by our issue, to make new alliances, and to mentor new leaders. We can become isolated as well if we have to spend a lot of time with the powerful or those representing the "other side" as part of our work or our fund-raising.

Advice: Touch base with your base often!

- **Becoming the problem:** Sad to say, but sometimes a group becomes so successful in their field that new ideas and leaders have difficulty getting heard and finding funding. They are told that so-and-so owns that issue. Or that funders have already made their commitments. Or that there isn't room at the table for them because that particular interest group's seat is already taken. Remember that no one has the answer; indeed, the more voices and hands at the table, the better the results.

    Advice: Insist that everyone have access to the table.

- **Captured by pod people:** Success sometimes makes leaders feel that their interests align with the powers that be, and they may come out against calls for change. Maybe the leader is personally benefiting from close connection with the powerful, or the group is too dependent on grants and contracts, or it is jealously protecting their position as THE spokesperson on their issue. If it's gone this far, personal tragedy or self-inflicted disgrace may be the only things that can reconnect a leader to their community.

    Advice: Practice self-reflection, make sure your circle of advisors isn't just yes-men and yes-women, and *listen* to others, especially if they raise doubts about your work.

Don't get the idea that I don't want you to succeed! I do! I set out all these warning signs to help you be aware of the challenges and rewards of leadership. Sort of like how "Rough Road Ahead" signs help you avoid crashing or damaging your car (or falling off your bike!). Throughout this book I've emphasized the need to be conscious and intentional in your life. Having the courage to jump in when others are hesitant, to act when you can't predict how things will turn out, and to put yourself out there despite the risks is certainly part of leadership. So is stepping back, asking others for advice, listening to the community, and examining your own motives and prejudices. What makes you an authentic and more whole human being is precisely what makes you a more effective and inspiring leader: humility, compassion, curiosity, and love for this place and its inhabitants.

CHAPTER 5 BLUEPRINT FOR CHANGE

In this chapter we went over how to move through conflict to achieve change, starting with the idea that there is much that even people from quite different backgrounds share that can form the basis of innovative and successful ways to address problems in our society. We also covered grounding our work in shared values, the importance of knowing what you hope to achieve, practicing ways to work well with others, and recognizing how both failure and success will offer you opportunities and challenges. I hope you've learned how to:

- Discover your community's most highly prized values.
- Drill down to discover values shared by your constituents and your opponents.
- Create goals that inspire, focus, and motivate action.
- Know how to ask for what you want.
- Use etiquette, kindness, and civility to promote your agenda.
- Splash on some vinegar when niceness is not enough to realize your goals.
- Formulate strategies to bring conflict to the surface and use it to your advantage.
- Find your BATNA (Best Alternative to a Negotiated Agreement).
- Master the challenges of failure AND success.

EPILOGUE

Thank you for joining me in this process of learning and discovery. In this book I've laid out the best personal and group strategies for successful leadership I know. I have shared methods that have worked for me in my thirty-plus years of activism—methods to engage and inspire others to help you make the change you hope for in the world. Through self-reflection we gain perspective and understanding of our place in the world, of what is important and what isn't. Authentic engagement with others—the whole wild and wonderfully diverse world of other people and cultures—brings deeper insight and knowledge to inform our activism so that we create a world that is more just, more secure, and more sustainable for all of us. Some ideas I've shared with you will help you deal with the challenges of running organizations without losing your optimism and maintain your sense of purpose and efficacy. You need all these to lead. I included stories from my experience and those of others that I hope resonated with you and helped illustrate my points.

E. B. White, the author of *Charlotte's Web*, wrote:

"If the world were merely seductive, that would be easy. If it were merely challenging, that would be no problem. But I arise in the morning torn between a desire to improve the world and a desire to enjoy the world. This makes it hard to plan the day."[11]

My own life has been an amazing journey. As a young man I never thought that I would someday be a leader. I love to read and have spent many happy hours inhabiting the worlds that great authors create. I also love walking in the woods and working in the garden.

To my surprise, I've learned to become a leader, drawn out of my inwardness by concern for the world and my desire to do something about it. Many teachers helped me along the way. A few in school, but many more were just "ordinary" people I met and befriended who opened my eyes to new ways of seeing. I have benefited especially from my family—my wife, whose love and talent with young children continually brings a child's fresh insight into my thinking; and my children, who got me down on my hands and knees to play with action figures and discover beetles and centipedes in the backyard when they were young and challenged me to recognize their humanity and agency when as young men they yearned to explore the world on their own terms.

Yet those who have torn me most effectively from my complacency are those whose lives and experiences differ most from mine, at least on the outside. Friends who fled war and famine. Friends who grew up on reservations. Friends who are stopped regularly by the police because of their skin color. Although I could never experience their lives in any meaningful way, their insights and cajoling broke down barriers of race, class, and education for me. It was their willingness to open their hearts to me that helped me most on my road to being a better leader.

My journey, my education, and my development as a leader aren't over. I learn more about leaders and leadership all the time, from people I work with, from books, and from classes I teach. By now I can recognize the signposts and read most of them. I expect to make a wrong turn every once in a while, but I know who to ask for help when I do. I hope that you have found some value in these thoughts and that they have helped put you on the path to becoming a leader yourself. Let

---

11. E. B. White, *Charlotte's Web* (New York: Harper & Brothers, 1952).

me know what you think, particularly what you found helpful and what you were looking for but did not find here. **Write me at rexburkholder@gmail.com with your ideas and stories. I look forward to hearing from you!**

ACKNOWLEDGMENTS

Who do you thank when the whole world has been your teacher? Of course, top of the list is Lydia, Gehron, and Lars, who give me hope, inspiration, and a wonderful time every time we get together, as well as a huge and ongoing lesson in what it means to love. My mom and dad for their guidance and insistence on living life responsibly and in service to the community. John Rehm for believing that I had something important to share and that I could actually get it on paper. Thank you as well to friends too numerous to count, who shared food and drink with me and discussed how we could solve the problems of the world. Then there is my friend and kayak partner, Matt Wuerker, who generously said yes when I asked him if he would draw the cover even though he was struggling to respond to the massacre of his fellow cartoonists at *Charlie Hebdo*. Thanks, Matt. Defend the rights of free speech: http://www.cartoonistsrights.org.

Thanks as well to the crew at Girl Friday Productions. Nancy Brandwein rightfully tore my manuscript into pieces and then put the puzzle back together again so that it made sense; thank you also, Nancy, for the great idea about creating a Leadership Resume. And much thanks to Ben Grossblatt, who checked my fuzzy memory and made sure I could tell the difference between *its* and *it's*. The handsome layout is Paul Barrett's.

It not only takes a village to raise a child, it also takes a village to make a book. Thanks to all.

ABOUT THE AUTHOR

Rex Burkholder trained as a biologist, working as a forester, recycler, and science teacher. Based in Portland, Oregon, he helped launch that city's bicycling revolution as a founder of the Bicycle Transportation Alliance. Burkholder also co-founded the Coalition for a Livable Future, breaking new ground in bringing together over one hundred diverse NGOs around issues of social and environmental justice. He served as a member of Portland's Metro Council from 2001–2013, leading efforts to reform regional transportation policy and integrate equity and climate change into operations and urban planning. Additionally, Burkholder has served on many key task forces and national boards, including Rail-volution and the Association of Metropolitan Planning Organizations. His work is recognized internationally and has taken him to countries in Latin America, Asia, and Europe to address sustainable transportation and climate change. In 2010, Burkholder was honored as a Global Ambassador for Ciclovia, an international movement to reclaim cities from the automobile.

For more information, visit Burkholder's blog at www.gettingto2100.org.

45196590R00101

Made in the USA
San Bernardino, CA
02 February 2017